NEET Young People and Training for Work
Learning on the margins

NEET Young People and Training for Work
Learning on the margins

*Robin Simmons and
Ron Thompson*

Trentham Books

Stoke on Trent, UK and Sterling, USA

Trentham Books Limited
Westview House   22883 Quicksilver Drive
734 London Road   Sterling
Oakhill   VA 20166-2012
Stoke on Trent   USA
Staffordshire
England ST4 5NP

First published 2011

British Library Cataloguing-in-Publication Data
A catalogue record for this book is available from the British Library

ISBN 978-1-85856-483-8

Cover image: *Broken Glass* by Jef Poskanzer
(used with thanks and full acknowledgement under Creative Commons Attribution 2.0 Generic Licence
http://commons.wikimedia.org/wiki/File:Broken_glass.jpg)

Designed and typeset by Trentham Books Ltd, Chester
Printed and bound in Great Britain by 4edge Limited, Hockley

This book is dedicated to our parents:
Alan and Brenda Simmons and Ronald
and Elizabeth Thompson

Contents

CONTENTS

Chapter 6
**The Tutors' Story: Professional practice
and pedagogy in E2E • 141**

Chapter 7
Conclusion: what does research say to policy? • 167

Acknowledgements

We would like to thank first of all our colleague Lisa Russell, whose ability as an ethnographer and unfailing enthusiasm for the E2E research provided a penetrating insight into the lives and experiences of a group of young people whose voice is rarely heard. We also wish to thank the young people themselves and the practitioners who worked with them, for their generosity in taking the time to share their views and experiences. Without their co-operation, this book could not have been written.

The ethnographic research on which this book is partly based was funded by the University of Huddersfield and the Consortium for Post-Compulsory Education and Training, and we are most grateful for their support. We would like to thank our colleagues at Huddersfield, particularly Roy Fisher, for their encouragement. We are grateful to the staff at Trentham Books, especially Gillian Klein for her guidance.

We would like to thank our wives, Dali and Margaret, for their patience and support during the many hours spent writing this book.

Preface

Young people not in education, employment or training (NEET) are the subject of extensive debate amongst policymakers, the media and other social commentators. Whilst youth unemployment is a matter of long-standing concern, NEET as a policy discourse expresses an increasing focus on education and training in tackling social exclusion and promoting economic competitiveness. Although the NEET category is a construct of policy approaches over the last fifteen years, it helps to highlight deep-seated problems facing young people, whose origin goes back much further.

This book explores three interrelated themes in understanding the lives of young people on the margins of work, education and training: the far-reaching social and economic changes that have radically altered the employment and educational opportunities available to young people; the policy context in which NEET young people have been constructed as responsible for their own predicament; and their lived experience as they negotiate provision aimed at re-engaging NEET young people. A central part of the book discusses findings from an ethnography of learners attending work-based learning programmes for marginalised young people; it shows how lived experience relates to and is influenced by the broader social and economic context, and the policy decisions made by successive governments.

We envisage that the book will appeal primarily to readers based in the United Kingdom but it is also of relevance to readers in North America and Australasia, as well as in Europe. Although the book focuses upon the experience of young people in England it also draws on literature from further afield. It engages with ideas and debates which have international relevance, particularly for those nations undergoing de-industrialisation and social change similar to that experienced in the UK.

We hope this book will be of value to students and lecturers on courses in youth work, social work, careers and guidance, as well as other courses which examine issues of social exclusion, such as sociology and social policy. The book will interest teachers and students on education studies and teacher training programmes, particularly those focused upon lifelong learning, and will be particularly useful for those interested in matters of social exclusion and social justice. Practitioners working with NEET young people and other excluded groups may also find the book illuminating.

1
Introduction

This book is about young people whose lives are profoundly affected by the conditions arising from social, political and economic change over a period of more than thirty years. It focuses on education and training provision for those on the margins of participation, often because of complex personal circumstances, which are themselves connected to transformations in the nature of work and society.

A large part of the book consists of a discussion of findings from an ethnographic study of 16 to 18-year-olds attending work-based learning programmes in the north of England. These findings concern the biographies, experiences and aspirations of the young people who took part in the research, and of the practitioners who supported their learning. However, it is not possible to do justice to ethnographic research without embedding it in a broader context, and the book ranges widely – dealing with the political economy of post-compulsory education, youth transitions from school to work and the contentious issue of young people not in education, employment or training (NEET).

This chapter introduces some of the key ideas and debates developed in more detail later, which illuminate our central concern: education and training provision for young people at risk of becoming – or remaining – NEET. It also provides an overview of our ethnographic research, locating it within a discussion of the characteristic features, advantages and limitations of ethnography.

Politicians of all major parties in the UK propose a central role for education in increasing social mobility and enabling young people to take their place in an employment market increasingly subject to global economic forces and the effects of technological progress. Although there is considerable debate about the extent to which a knowledge economy has displaced more routine forms of employment, few would contest the assertion that educational achievement is a pre-requisite for an increasing proportion of jobs. The lives of most people are greatly influenced by the type of waged labour they are able to undertake, and in both political and public debate a growing focus on purely economic benefits competes with more traditional views of education as having intrinsic value. To some extent, liberal notions of education as an induction to certain ways of thinking and feeling – inseparable from the individual and contributing to a common cultural heritage – have been displaced by a view of education as a commodity, something to be bought and sold as occasion demands.

From either perspective, education is seen as both a private and a public good, as having the power to transform lives and promote social cohesion. In such conceptions, access and participation are central goals, and the problem of education is largely to do with opportunity. Since the end of the Second World War, various policy initiatives have aimed to extend the fruits of education to a greater proportion of young people and, at least on the surface, have enjoyed much success – often assisted by economic, social and cultural change. The period of compulsory education has lengthened – to 15 in 1947 and 16 in 1972 – and participation in post-compulsory education has dramatically increased (see Figure 1.1). By 2015, all young people will be required to engage in some form of education or training up to the age of 18, a New Labour policy re-affirmed by the Conservative-Liberal Democrat coalition which came to power after the 2010 general election.

Although the idea of education as a progressive force continues to dominate – and perhaps rightly so – the *process* of education has been subject to extensive critique, particularly from writers working in Marxist, feminist and critical race theory traditions. These perspectives reveal that apparently neutral or empowering institutions are deeply implicated in processes of domination through which ruling elites reproduce themselves, and those in subservient positions are kept in

2

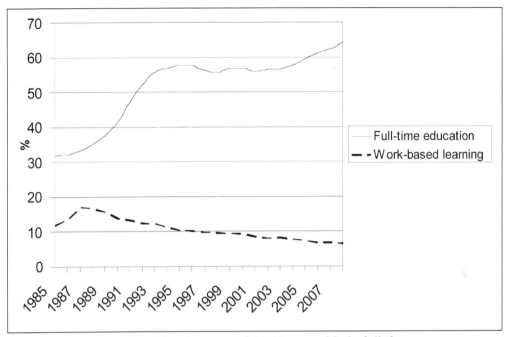

Figure 1.1: Participation rate of 16-18 year olds in full-time education, 1985-2008

(Source: Statistical First Release SFR 18/2010 (DfE, 2010a)

check. Louis Althusser (1971) proposed that education helps to maintain dominant ideologies, and Pierre Bourdieu (1974:32) wrote that 'It is probably cultural inertia which still makes us see education in terms of the ideology of the school as a liberating force ... even when the indications tend to be that it is one of the most effective means of perpetuating the existing social pattern'.

According to such critiques, the content and structure of education express the power of dominant groups to determine the value society attributes to different forms of knowledge, and to distribute such knowledge in ways that serve to maintain their position. When combined with postmodern perspectives which question the very possibility of knowledge in an absolute sense, the idea of education as passing on neutral truths of value to all looks increasingly untenable. The problem of education, then, becomes *who* learns *what* as well as enabling greater access.

Educational systems are at least partly an expression of a society's dominant values, culture and politics. In the UK, the closing decades of the twentieth century and the opening decade of the twenty-first are regarded by some as a single political era, in which continuities between periods of Conservative and Labour administration are part of the broader international hegemony of neo-liberalism. According to this view, the focus of New Labour on issues such as social exclusion and policies of limited redistribution did not constitute a break with the principles underlying the more confrontational approach that characterised Thatcherism, and the assumptions and values informing New Labour were not fundamentally different from their Conservative predecessors or, indeed, their Coalition successors. Writing in *New Left Review*, Perry Anderson argues that centre-left 'Third Way' regimes which preserve a compassionate public authority in an attempt to ameliorate the effects of market policies are 'the best ideological shell of capitalism today' (Anderson, 2000:7), and perpetuate the dominance of market philosophies in economic and political life. However, even within the same broad framework, different policy emphases can have significant effects on the most vulnerable individuals. This book explores the ways in which specific conceptualisations of economy and state are realised in the lives of young people.

The New Labour years were associated with increased public funding for certain areas of learning – such as adult basic skills and vocational training – and initiatives aimed at widening participation, including post-16 curriculum change and the Educational Maintenance Allowance. At the same time, however, the combination of political centralisation and market-based reforms characteristic of neo-liberal approaches to public sector provision were taken over from Thatcherism and even intensified, increasing social stratification in all sectors of education (Ball, 2003). As in other parts of the public sector, a hard core of market-based policies was softened by subsidiary concessions to improved services and a focus on social inclusion. More recently, the Coalition Government has surrounded further encroachments of marketisation and privatised delivery in education with notions of fairness, equal opportunity and social mobility. The underlying philosophy is one of individualism, in which people are held responsible for their own success or failure; inequalities in the resources necessary to succeed in education are overlooked. Whilst participation – whether in education and training or in paid employment – is presented as a primary goal of intrinsic value, this is to be achieved largely through re-forming psychological dispositions and aspirations. Exclusion from education or employment is attributed to deficiencies in individuals and communities, and policies intended to raise participation are based on a carrot and stick approach in which increased access and support is combined with welfare to work measures.

NEET or not?

The New Labour slogan 'Education, education, education' typifies an approach in which supply-side initiatives, aimed at fitting people for work, are seen as *the* legitimate arena for state intervention and resources, whilst policies aimed at increasing the demand for labour are largely ruled out. Globalisation, it is claimed, leaves no alternative, for if the workforce becomes too expensive, employers will simply take their business elsewhere. For young people in particular, this leads to a situation in which periods of job shortage and shifts in the structure of the labour market create a scramble for qualifications. Credential inflation nullifies many of the benefits of educational expansion, and the lowest achievers are increasingly differentiated from their more fortunate peers. Now, 'sixteen-year-olds who insist that they want proper jobs and who try to avoid all alternatives have become a new problem group' (Roberts, 2009a:358).

The history of the NEET category highlights global economic and social trends which affect young people as they leave school and begin to construct an adult life. The demise of large-scale industry in many parts of the UK has led to greater fragmentation of young people's experiences as collective transitions from school to factory or mine were replaced by jobs with smaller service-based employers, and the increasing participation in post-compulsory education evident from Figure 1.1 was as much the result of diminished opportunities elsewhere as of curriculum and institutional change within education.

Throughout the 1980s and early 1990s, full-time education or a place on a youth training scheme gradually became established for the majority of school leavers, comprising 68 per cent of 16 to 18-year-olds in 1994 compared with 44 per cent a decade earlier (DfE, 2010a). Young people who rejected these options came under increasing pressure, and in 1988 their entitlement to unemployment benefit was removed. This measure promoted full-time education or training as the desired post-16 progression route; the unemployed young person ceased to exist, and was replaced with a recalcitrant youth who was outside education and employment. Paradoxically, a measure aimed at persuading more young people to remain in education actually made them more difficult to reach. As officials and youth researchers quickly found, these young people could disappear from the radar of state surveillance and, apart from information on their total numbers, little was known about the specific nature and characteristics of this group until the pioneering study of unemployed young people by Istance *et al* (1994).

It is difficult to know anything about NEET young people as a group because their circumstances are too disparate. The category is defined in terms of what young people are not, rather than what they are. Generalisations are therefore problematic, and it is not even possible to say that being NEET is a negative status for all young people. For example, motherhood or travelling during a gap year are valued by many, and seeking employment in preference to certain forms of post-16 study or training is sometimes a rational decision. Nevertheless, many studies have highlighted that being NEET is likely to have negative consequences in later life, is structured along familiar lines of class and gender, and is often just one facet of broader experiences of deprivation for young people living in disadvantaged communities. Except in a few specific circumstances, being NEET is something best avoided; the problem for many young people is to work out how this can be achieved.

Individualisation, structural inequality and social reproduction

Ulrich Beck (1992) proposes that societies throughout the world are undergoing a process of individualisation, in which social conditions are experienced in an increasingly differentiated way from person to person. According to this view, traditional patterns and arrangements in work and society are weakening, and collective experiences of class, gender and culture are being replaced by unique biographies and ambitions, alongside a greater reliance on individual's own resources to achieve personal goals and avoid undesired outcomes. However, Beck is clear that such processes do not mean the end of social inequality, because access to resources – economic, social or cultural – significantly influences both individual aspirations and the chances of attaining them. What he suggests is that, whilst the structure of social inequality in post-industrial societies is remarkably stable, inequality is no longer perceived and confronted as a class question, and individual-level solutions compete with collective responses to the risks caused by post-industrial life. Consequently, inequalities are recast in terms of how individuals respond to the challenges facing them and the steps they take to avoid future risks. Social problems, such as unemployment, ill-health and crime come to be seen in the light of individual dispositions and inadequacies, or as the outcome of perverse lifestyle choices. Trends such as globalisation, the weakening of family and community structures, and decreasing confidence in science and traditional forms of authority all confront individuals with a range of options and disrupt their capacity for joining in collective action. Old certainties around class, family, neighbourhood and identity are replaced with increasingly complex individual histories, in which a person's life becomes a reflexive biographical project whose success or failure is their own responsibility.

It is important to distinguish between individualisation as a product of capitalism – and therefore as a process to be critiqued – and discourses which use individualisation to justify individual-level solutions to social inequality (Thompson, 2011a). Indeed, since the late 1970s, participation in education and training has increasingly been conceived as the most effective way of reducing unemployment. Factors which contribute to disengagement, such as disaffection or limited aspirations, are regarded as inherent to young people and their families, rather than as part of a complex interplay between individual dispositions and other factors, including structural inequalities, identities constructed within family and community, and contingent events.

Research with NEET young people indicates that they often attribute their status to individualised factors such as their low ability, lack of work experience, and low confidence or self-esteem. Social exclusion is a normal part of life for many of them, and does not immediately strike them in terms of class or its intersection with gender and ethnicity. Furthermore, the jobs that young people do or the lifestyle choices they make have, to some extent, eroded class and gender segregation; service employment, higher education institutions, and certain cultural events attract young people from a broad range of backgrounds. However, class, gender and ethnic patterns in youth transitions have not disappeared or become irrelevant (Furlong, 2009). What has changed is the way young people deal with situations structured by inequality. Their approaches to education, employment or consumption have diversified and fragmented. Furlong and Cartmel (2007) refer to the increasing disconnection between objective and subjective experiences as the *epistemological fallacy* of late modernity. They observe that 'People's life chances remain highly structured at the same time as they increasingly seek solutions on an individual, rather than a collective basis' (p5). According to this account, processes of individualisation and reflexive modernisation (Lash, 1992) have obscured, but not obliterated, the role of social and economic structures in shaping the life course.

Educational and social privilege continue to go hand-in-hand (Roberts, 2009a); increases in participation rates and educational markets make little difference to those already occupying elite sections of schooling and higher education. Even credential inflation is less corrosive for those who can attain the highest grades and supplement their formal qualifications with broader forms of cultural capital. More generally, it is well understood that educational achievement and participation in higher education decline markedly with decreasing social class. Although precisely what is meant by class and the relative importance of occupational, economic and cultural factors in its construction is debatable, the broad patterns are clear. To be born into a working-class family is to have a significantly lower chance of success in increasingly competitive education and employment markets. Reforms over the last twenty years which have claimed to address class-based educational inequality have tended to have the opposite effect (Ball, 2006), channelling the families with the sharpest elbows into relatively elite areas of state provision. As a result, low-status forms of educational establishment – neighbourhood comprehensive schools, FE colleges and certain forms of work-based learning – tend to be disproportionately populated by young people from lower social classes, or to be at best second-chance institutions for the middle class.

The effects of race and gender are more complex. Gillborn (2010) argues that race and class inequalities cannot be fully understood in isolation, and intersectionality – the exploration of lived experience as constructed simultaneously through classed, raced and gendered subjectivities and structures – has been increasingly prominent in recent work in the sociology of education. However, in quantitative terms, educational inequalities of race and gender are second-order effects compared with social class (Moore, 2004:15; Heath, 2000). The variations between classes are greater than the variations between the genders or different ethnic groups – and this is why it has been relatively straightforward to reduce differences in educational achievement between (for example) girls and boys whilst those between the highest and lowest social classes persist. Nevertheless, deterministic ascriptions of life chances to whole sections of society can be misleading, and differences within groups are just as important as those between groups. Educational achievement is just one amongst many factors producing inequality and, particularly in relation to gender and ethnicity, cultural norms and expectations still tend to channel young people into traditional occupational and social roles.

Although processes of individualisation have made young people's biographies less predictable and increasingly diversified, their prospects are still profoundly influenced by their location in a matrix of class, gender and race positions. Social reproduction, the process by which relations of dominance and subordination in society are perpetuated, continues to operate, even though the rhetoric of successive governments on equal opportunity and social mobility suggests otherwise. The role of education in the process of social reproduction, and particularly the ways in which post-compulsory education and training for disadvantaged young people tend to reinforce their position, is a central theme of this book.

Work-based learning and Entry to Employment

For adults, work-based learning tends to be associated with learning opportunities in the workplace – often with a view to formal accreditation and connected with specific job roles (Avis, 2004:197). Work-based learning for young people, however, tends to be associated with social control. Although apprenticeships often lead to recognised vocational qualifications and progression to higher levels, other forms of work-based learning for young people have tended to operate as either work substitution programmes or extensions of schooling, attempting to compensate for a shrinking youth labour market, a history of educational disadvantage, or both.

At their peak in the 1980s, programmes such as the Youth Training Scheme (YTS) catered for a significant proportion of 16 to 18-year-olds (see Figure 1.1). More recently, however, compensatory work-based learning has been increasingly marginalised as participation in full-time general education has become the norm for school leavers, and by 2008 less than six per cent of this cohort was in work-based learning (Russell *et al*, 2011). Such programmes are now primarily aimed at re-integrating those seen as disaffected or disengaged from schooling (Thompson, 2011b), and are often regarded as the most suitable alternative to full-time education for many young people, whose disengagement is attributed to a non-academic disposition (Thomson and Russell, 2009). The description 'work-based' is used to denote the characteristics of teaching and learning rather than location, although work placements provided voluntarily by local businesses are often an important feature of the curriculum.

The idea of more practical, vocationally-based approaches to learning is attractive in a number of ways and is often promoted as a way of including young people who have failed in (or been failed by) conventional schooling. However, certain forms of work-based learning may also exclude young people in a number of ways, not least from principled, conceptual knowledge. Avis (2004:212) argues that, although the interest of young people in vocational learning should be acknowledged, they should have access to forms of knowledge that allow them to understand and critique the practices and disciplines of the workplace. Similarly, Wheelahan (2009) suggests that competence-based training denies access to the knowledge required for full participation in society. Furthermore, although compensatory work-based learning is often notable for high levels of care and individual attention for young people, Ecclestone (2009) regards these programmes as potentially reinforcing dependency, and sees them as largely replacing knowledge with the construction of what she calls a 'vulnerable self', requiring continued intervention from practitioners.

Entry to Employment (E2E), the work-based learning programme discussed in this book, illustrates these tensions and contradictions. Introduced in England in 2003 following the Cassels Report (DfES, 2001), the programme was originally conceived as a stepping stone to an apprenticeship. E2E was intended for 16 to 18-year-olds unable to progress into education or employment because of poor basic skills, low motivation and self-esteem, or a history of behavioural problems. In the prevailing discourse, such traits and dispositions are termed 'barriers to learning', and although policy documents often recognised that such barriers may be traced back to structural inequalities, E2E took an essentially individual-level approach of building skills and attempting to eliminate deficits. The programme attempted to re-engage young people through a curriculum containing three main strands: personal and social development, basic skills and vocational learning.

E2E contained a number of progressive elements, such as an emphasis on the individual and a broad developmental ethos, and was not driven by a narrow focus on acquiring work-related qualifications. However, it suffered from low status, was strongly classed and gendered, and as Simmons (2009) argues, could not provide access to the kinds of powerful knowledge called for by Avis and Wheelahan. As part of a shift towards programmes delivering more measurable outcomes, including recognised qualifications in basic skills and other, vocationally-relevant areas, in late 2010 E2E was incorporated into a broader curriculum framework known as Foundation Learning (DCSF, 2010). Although this ended E2E as a discrete provision, the new framework adopts similar approaches to re-engaging young people through work-based learning. The models of knowledge and assumptions about young people encountered in Foundation Learning are little different to those in E2E.

Ethnography: a distinctive analytical mentality

Ethnography is distinguished by a naturalistic approach, in which the researcher becomes involved in people's lives for an extended period of time, studying their actions and expressions in everyday settings. Ethnography is interpretive, attempting to understand the often conflicting perspectives of participants. Although there are many variations on the form taken by ethnographies (Walford, 2009), they usually have a number of characteristic features. A wide range of data is collected, with participant observation and relatively informal interviews or conversations being the main approaches but also including photographs, artefacts and documentary evidence. Data collection and interpretation is usually flexible, iterative and initially unstructured; in most ethnographies, an inductive approach is taken in which the research design is relatively open at the outset, and is refined in the light of emerging data (Hammersley and Atkinson, 2007).

In some ways, ethnography is controversial. Its rationale is embedded in a critique of quantitative social research, particularly where large-scale surveys or controlled experiments claim to parallel the methods of natural science. Ethnography challenges these approaches on a number of grounds, arguing that the validity of quantitative research – and also some forms of qualitative research – is compromised by limitations such as lack of transferability from controlled to natural settings, a reliance on what people say rather than what they are observed to do, and a neglect of individual agency in preference to overall behavioural trends. By contrast, ethnography claims to capture social processes and the meanings underlying them, producing theoretically informed descriptions which 'remain close to the concrete reality of particular events, but at the same time reveal general features of human social life' (Hammersley, 1992:12).

This twofold claim about ethnography raises questions about the nature of the knowledge it generates. Firstly, how can descriptions of a particular concrete reality contribute to the development of general accounts of social processes – that is, to the development of theory, in some sense of the word? Although ethnographers are usually cautious about moving from knowledge of particular contexts to broader claims, the relationship between ethnography and theory has been extensively debated (Hammersley, 1992; Brewer, 2000). Whilst some authors aim to develop abstract propositions which explain certain aspects of the social world, others have more modest ambitions, seeking to investigate the particular features of a specific case. In this context, the idea that ethnography produces 'thick descriptions' (Geertz, 1975) has been used to bridge the gap between particularity and generality, referring to an approach in which theoretical analysis is closely interwoven with rich description. Here, the aim is not to generate theory but to use existing theory in order to understand more fully the social meanings of a particular situation for its participants.

The second question raised by ethnography's claim to reveal the general through the particular is whether the idea of a concrete reality, to be captured by ethnographic methods, is at all sustainable. The origins of ethnography in nineteenth-century anthropological research provided an underlying ideology in which the researcher was seen as external (and, by implication, superior) to the culture being studied – a naïve realism in which detached observers produce objective and un-ambiguous descriptions. Today, ethnographers recognise that the values and interests of the researcher cannot be separated from the investigative process, highlighting the need to reflexively consider the impact of the researcher's own standpoint. Ethnography is just as much a social and cultural phenomenon as the cases it sets out to investigate, and it cannot be assumed that ethnographers, as socially embedded individuals, can arrive at complete and unarguable reproductions of a social reality.

Although it is clear that ethnographic descriptions are socially con-structed and therefore liable to error and bias, the alternative is not simply to retreat into relativism, in which no account can be better than another. Hammersley (1992) and Denzin and Lincoln (1998) propose more subtle forms of realism, which assume that, although knowledge is socially produced, the phenomena it describes exist independently of our claims about them and can be represented more or less accurately by these claims. Furthermore, they propose that reasonably objective criteria exist for choosing between competing claims, such as com-patibility with other well-established claims, and the nature and robust-ness of the evidence. Although social inquiry cannot reproduce reality, it can represent it with some degree of completeness and credibility. The particular viewpoint of the researcher will make certain features relevant and others irrelevant, and there can be multiple, non-contradictory and valid descriptions of the same phenomenon (Hammersley, 1992:51).

Researching E2E: an ethnography of work-based learning
The ethnography discussed in this book took place between September 2008 and June 2009, and explored the experiences of young people and practitioners involved in E2E programmes in two neighbouring local

13

authorities in northern England. Following the discussion above, which highlights the positioning, values and cultural background of the researcher in ethnographic enquiry, it will prove helpful to give a brief indication of the origins of this project and the values informing it. The initial impetus came from the experience of the authors in working with E2E tutors who were following initial teacher training courses at our university, particularly through teaching assessments in which we spent time with tutors, talking to them about their work and observing their teaching. This led to an interest in the young people attending E2E provision. How were their lives, education and future prospects affected by a programme aiming to redress earlier educational disadvantage? It appeared to us that there was a real dilemma in this provision, in that the difficult circumstances in which many of the young people found themselves seemed to demand specialist intervention, yet the very separateness and particular nature of E2E posed the risk that it would reinforce negative experiences and contribute to further exclusion and inequality.

If ethnography is about telling stories (Walford, 2009), then here was a story demanding to be told, one that would require close involvement over a period of time with people in many different roles: learners, tutors, managers and careers advisers, to name just a few. The central questions we hoped to answer were: who are the young people following E2E, and what has led to their involvement with the programme? What do they learn in E2E, and how? Where does it lead? What are the backgrounds of the practitioners working with them and how do they see their role? With the support of the university, we were able to appoint an experienced ethnographer, Lisa Russell, to conduct the fieldwork. Lisa shared with the authors a concern with social justice and a desire to tell the story of young people on the margins of education, and had just completed research on alternative provision for young people excluded from school – an investigation which had brought her into contact with E2E programmes and the learners attending them.

E2E operated as a partnership in the two local authorities, which we refer to as *Middlebridge* and *Greenford*. Middlebridge has a population of approximately 400,000 and comprises two large post-industrial towns, together with smaller towns and villages, whilst Greenford is centred on one major town and its satellites, and has a population of around 200,000. Although service industries have replaced much of the industrial base, manufacturing continues to provide significant employment, accounting for around 20 per cent of the local workforce in 2009. Both authorities are ethnically diverse, although there is considerable geographic variation in the representation of different ethnic groups, some areas being almost exclusively white whilst others have large ethnic minority communities. Overall, 84 per cent of the population in Middlebridge are of white British ethnicity, with the largest ethnic minority groups being of Pakistani or Indian descent. The proportion of ethnic minorities in Greenford is somewhat smaller, with 10 per cent being non-white, mainly of Pakistani descent. During the research, which took place during the recession following the financial crisis of 2008, the area saw a significant increase in the number of people claiming Jobseeker's allowance, from 2.5 per cent of the working-age population in mid-2008 to nearly 5 per cent by June 2009. However, there was little change in NEET rates, which remained at around 9.5 per cent in Middlebridge and 8.5 per cent in Greenford (Russell *et al*, 2011).

The research explored the experiences of learners and practitioners and consisted of two phases. The first phase comprised an initial exploration and mapping of E2E provision, which operated as a partnership across both authorities led by a local further education (FE) college, and comprising a range of private and voluntary providers. An important feature of the research at this stage was an initial survey of providers, in which Lisa spent extended periods of time in the company of Connexions personal advisers as they visited different organisations and talked to tutors and individual young people. This was followed by interviews with managers and practitioners working in the Connexions service and in E2E providers, and analysis of key documents at local and national level. The second and most important phase of the research involved a detailed ethnographic investigation of four case-study sites selected from the partnership to encompass a range of different types of E2E provider, in terms of the experiences offered to young people and the orientation of the training.

Middlebridge College is a large FE college whose main campus is near the centre of Middlebridge; it offers a wide range of courses to young people and mature students. The E2E provision did not have a specific vocational focus, offering instead a broad programme aimed at increasing confidence and self-esteem, whilst also helping to develop literacy and numeracy skills. Progression from E2E to other courses in the college was regarded as a strength of the provision.

Action for Youth is a voluntary organisation which operates in two locations in Middlebridge. It offers training in engineering, motor vehicle maintenance and construction, and most staff members have a background within these industries. Young people following the E2E programme were developing vocational skills and engaging in projects, outdoor pursuits and residential activities.

One of the private-sector providers, *MGC Training*, offered experience and vocational qualifications in childcare, care of the elderly, warehousing and retail. Programmes such as sport and fitness or health and beauty were also offered as a way of developing personal skills.

Aim for Work, another private provider, offered a programme of work placements and tasters combined with vocational qualifications, mainly in administration, retail and warehousing. Both providers claimed to have close links with local employers, which they regarded as having particular value in obtaining work placements and job opportunities for learners. As might be expected, E2E programmes in the more specialist providers were highly gendered along traditional vocational lines.

Fieldwork took place between November 2008 and May 2009, involving 87 hours of participant observation and 63 semi-structured interviews with young people, tutors, Connexions staff, and managers of E2E provision. Five interviews were unrecorded at the request of participants, whilst the remainder were tape-recorded and transcribed. Most interviews were on a one-to-one basis; however, three took place with two learners and one with three learners. Field notes and photographs recorded learning activities and teaching styles, aspects of the learning environment, the behaviour of young people and their interactions with staff, and how space and time were utilised.

The distinctive nature of an ethnographic approach combines a rich and detailed exploration of people's perspectives and activities with a more detached and critical analysis which seeks to understand a culture or community, including relations within the culture and with the outside world. This enabled us to explore the complex nature of E2E provision and relate it more broadly to education and training. An ethnographic approach provided a fuller picture than would be possible through interviews alone, particularly where learners and learning activities were concerned. The following extract from Lisa's field notes provides some flavour of the engagement made possible by an ethnographic approach, as well as giving an insight into the experiences of E2E learners which will be explored in later chapters.

> **9.30am** I arrive. Fran, Susanna and Steve [E2E tutors] are in their office. Some of the learners are on computers. Fran is printing off price tags for the Christmas Card Fair and cutting them out. They are selling large cards for £1.25 and smaller ones for £1. They have made around 90 cards. They have also made gift tags, packs of ten which they will sell for 50p.
>
> I enter the hall where the card sale is taking place. There are stalls all around and tables and chairs in the centre. Kyle and Chris [E2E learners] are behind the stall table; both have their MP3 players and packets of sweets. Kyle wears his hat and beige coat; he has one red glove and one cerise glove. Chris is wearing his green and yellow tracksuit. Both wear trainers. They have neatly set out the stand, fan-displaying all the cards. They have made some birthday cards and anniversary cards. There is Christmas music in the background. Kyle and Chris joke about being glad they brought their MP3 players.
>
> Susanna explains that all the Foundation Learning students are here. She says they were not invited to take part in the fair, although they asked if they could. [She says this with some resentment, implying that they feel excluded from the college.] Most of the other students involved in the fair have learning difficulties. Susanna says that the money raised by these other students will go towards a minibus and that the money raised by E2E learners will be used to take them on a trip. Susanna says that getting involved with activities such as this is easier in a college; setting up such an activity in a private provider would be much more complex. I ask Kyle and Chris what they would like to do on their outing, both say go-karting. A suggestion box for learners has been placed in the E2E classroom.
>
> Susanna suggests that I get a visitor pass today as there will be a lot of people coming and going and senior staff may pay a visit. She walks me over to the college entrance, we go outside for this. It is a fair distance [from] where E2E is. The E2E learners are physically separated from the main goings-on in the college.
>
> ...

When we return some people have started to enter the hall. The fair starts at 10.30am. The other stalls sell plants, bulbs, bric-a-brac, food and the like, there is a raffle and one girl goes round with a jar of sweets, 20p to guess how many sweets. Susanna says they are not located in the best spot, the majority of people arrive and move towards the café, meaning the E2E stall is visited last. Susanna comments on how their lack of Christmas card sales may be attributed to college politics [OC another hint about how E2E staff feel about being part of the college].

11.10am Kyle and Chris disappear (they leave early, although Susanna said they need to go into class) and Jack and another [learner, new to the course] take up a seat behind the stall. Jack actively tries to sell the cards, he says 'I can do you a deal' and talks to customers. I say he is good at this and he says he is used to talking to people as he often rings big firms for his brother's company. Susanna says, 'I didn't know that'. He says 'Yeah, I'm used to it'.

They have sold around 20 cards and made about £20. Jack offers to try to sell some of the cards in the staff rooms and corridors. He goes away with some cards and gift tags, but fails to sell any more. Susanna says they will try to sell the rest in packs later in the week.

(10 December 2008; OC = Observer Comment)

Table 1.1 shows the distribution across the four case-study sites of the learners interviewed, in terms of gender and ethnicity. Table 1.2 shows the pseudonyms used in this book for the young people and practitioners who took part in the research, whether or not they were interviewed. The names of female participants are emboldened. Interviews were arranged through tutors and managers at the case-study sites and were normally conducted as part of a longer visit including observations, documentary analysis and interviews with staff.

Table 1.1: Learners interviewed, by gender, ethnicity and case-study site

	Gender		Ethnicity			Total
	M	F	White	Asian	Mixed Heritage	
Middlebridge College	10	4	10	1	3	**14**
Action for Youth	16	1	14	2	1	**17**
MGC Training	0	9	8	1	0	**9**
Aim for Work	3	8	9	2	0	**22**
Total	**29**	**22**	**41**	**6**	**4**	**51**

Learners					Practitioners	
Middlebridge College	Kyle	Chris	**Ellie**	Alan	**Fran**	**Susanna**
	Lewis	Kyle	Chris	Philip	Steve	**Carol**
	Daniel	Darren	**Shannon**	Adam		
	Emma	**Charlotte**	Leon	Jack		
	Shoaib	Patrick				
Action for Youth	Kieran	Usman	Rob	Nick	**Gillian**	George
	Diana	Majid	Luke	Carl	John	Ian
	Aidan	Joseph	Phil	Thomas	Dave	
	Conal	Mike	Tom	Jason		
	Geoffrey					
MGC Training	**Janice**	**Kerry**	**Amanda**	**Yafiah**	**Liz**	**Sarah**
	Faye	**Jade**	**Danielle**	**Donna**	**Linda**	**Jenny**
	Ruth					
Aim for Work	**Hannah**	Matt	**Linzi**	**Aisha**	**Tara**	
	Becky	**Nasreen**	**Sophie**	**Mary**	**Leanne**	
	Sean	**Jessica**	Carl			
Connexions Service/Other Providers	Alice	Alfie			**Alison**	Martyn
					Kelly	
					Josh	**Gwyneth**

Table 1.2: Participants in the E2E research project

Outline of the book

The plan of the book is first to examine the broad context of education, employment and training for young people aged 16-19, providing a background against which the particular issues relating to young people on the margins of participation are discussed. Chapters 2 and 3 take up some of the themes introduced in this chapter, exploring the nature of post-compulsory education and its socio-economic context, with a particular focus on the English FE system and the underpinning discourses of globalisation, knowledge economy and social inclusion. Chapter 2 explains why participation in education and training has become such a central part of the policies of successive governments, and discusses the limitations of such policies in a political environment which sees competitive markets as the main avenue towards better lives for all. Against this backdrop, Chapter 3 explores the changing nature of youth transitions, arguing that whilst post-school experiences have become more complex and protracted, individual agency is constrained by structural factors in the economy and society.

In Chapter 4, the specific issue of NEET young people is examined in detail, and a range of empirical evidence is reviewed which casts light on the experiences and prospects of young people in this category. The chapter highlights some of the benefits and limitations of constructing NEET as a problem status, weighing the contrasting effects of the intense public and political focus on these young people, for example the benefits of increased resources for interventions or the stigma often attached to non-participation. Many commentators have pointed out that the NEET category collects together a disparate group of young people, and we explore some of the main sub-groups and the interventions that have been used to increase and sustain participation. We also review the evidence on factors which lead to an increased risk of becoming NEET, and on the effects in later life of extended periods of exclusion. We draw on the biographies of some of the young people who participated in the E2E project, and show that they are 'ordinary people' (Russell *et al*, 2011) not dissimilar to working-class teenagers elsewhere in education or employment.

Chapters 5 and 6 focus more specifically on Entry to Employment programmes. Using ethnographic data from the E2E project, Chapter 5 describes the curricula, environments and learning experiences of young people in the four case study sites, highlighting the achievements of learners and tutors but also the constraints and limitations which operate in E2E providers. Issues such as the marginalisation of E2E provision, the largely generic nature of the curriculum, and the difficulty of meaningful progression are highlighted. In Chapter 6, we turn our attention to the practitioners who work with the young people, exploring the biographies, practices and discourses of tutors and other practitioners working in E2E. The concluding chapter draws together the main themes of the book, critically appraising its arguments and findings. It considers alternative approaches to engaging NEET young people, arguing that effective interventions require not only reshaping practice but also radical changes in the way society and economy are structured.

2

Knowledge, Economy and
Social Exclusion

The lives of young people are complex. The challenges and opportunities they face derive partly from individual agency, local circumstances, and their own characteristics and dispositions. However, even decisions and choices which appear to be individual do not take place in a vacuum. The life chances of any individual or group are shaped and structured to a significant degree by broader social and economic change and by the ways in which knowledge and education are conceptualised. This chapter provides an overview of some of the key socio-economic changes of the past thirty years and discusses how these changes have affected the contexts in which young people live.

We begin by explaining how globalisation, or at least its dominant neo-liberal interpretations, provides the backdrop for a broad range of policy decisions in the UK, but especially policies which relate to education and training. The chapter argues that young people today inhabit an environment in which dominant understandings of work, the economy and the relationship of education to individual success and social well-being are increasingly shaped by particular neo-liberal understandings of political economy. It explains how the current emphasis on workforce knowledge and skills has taken root in the UK, and discusses how the notion of employability is related to the labour market and the inequalities within it. The chapter concludes by developing three inter-related themes: the increasing individualisation of social and economic relations; patterns of social exclusion in the UK; and the various strategies that have attempted to promote social inclusion by integrating marginalised young people into the world of work.

Globalisation and social change

Although there is no agreed definition of globalisation, certain key principles broadly constitute this phenomenon. Whilst globalisation is a contested and sometimes chaotic concept, it can still be used heuristically to help understand and explain social change. Globalisation is generally understood to describe the idea that the world is becoming increasingly interconnected and that traditional divisions between nation states are breaking down. Economic, cultural and political connectivity are all increasing, accompanied by growth in the flow of goods, services, people and ideas across the world. Arguably, this is accompanied by a decline in the importance of geographical and national boundaries, and increasing interdependence between countries and people. Finance, knowledge and information can move around the world quickly and efficiently. Time and space are seen to be compressed, especially through the use of information technology and fast, relatively inexpensive forms of travel (Lauder *et al*, 2006:30-31).

In many societies, and particularly in English-speaking nations such as the UK and the USA, globalisation is often presented as driving profound, almost revolutionary change. Established norms and values are portrayed as outdated: the need for creative and innovative ways of thinking and acting is emphasised, whether in relation to broad economic and political questions, employment or education policies, or everyday issues such as patterns of leisure or consumption. According to official discourse, economic success and social well-being rest upon the ability of governments, organisations and individuals to adapt and respond rapidly to the ever-increasing forces of globalisation (Avis, 2007). Resistance to change, particularly if based upon traditional notions of social solidarity, such as trade unionism or other forms of class-based politics, is increasingly seen as not just old-fashioned but inappropriate. For the UK's major political parties, as well as much of the mainstream media, the nation's success or failure hinges largely on its ability to compete in a global marketplace. Hence, long-standing concerns about the UK's economic performance and the efficacy of its education and training systems are endowed with greater urgency by the rise of China, India and other so-called emerging economies.

Claims about the impact of globalisation, and the need for urgent responses, must be treated with some caution and scepticism. Although certain quantitative and qualitative changes have occurred, globalisation cannot be regarded as an entirely new phenomenon. It is perhaps more accurate to describe the social and economic changes associated with globalisation as representing an intensification of long-standing patterns of trade, competition and migration rather than as a decisive break with the past. Furthermore, whilst dominant discourses on globalisation draw on some objective changes, they also promote subjective dimensions as objective processes.

Education and the neo-liberal state

In the UK, neo-liberal understandings about the nature of globalisation have led to far-reaching changes in the way society is organised. Although its roots can be traced back to the classical liberalism of the nineteenth century and the revival of liberal ideology in Europe during the 1940s and 1950s, neo-liberalism in the UK emerged during the economic crisis of the early 1970s and the rise to power of Margaret Thatcher's Conservative Government at the end of that decade. The 1973 OPEC oil crisis, combined with increasing inflation and rising levels of unemployment – especially amongst young people – meant that, by the mid-1970s, the UK's relative economic decline was becoming increasingly apparent. Against this backdrop, in 1976, the Labour Government sought to buttress an ailing economy with support from the International Monetary Fund (IMF). In many ways this marked a turning point for the nation: the conditions imposed by the IMF in return for its loan required the UK to begin a programme of economic restructuring. Thereafter, the post-war social democratic settlement began to crumble.

In the decades after the war, the role of education in producing the human capital which would allow UK industry and commerce to compete internationally was increasingly emphasised. Such concerns began to intensify during the crisis of capital in the 1970s. From this time onwards the perceived shortcomings of educational institutions, teachers and young people have increasingly been seen as the cause of a range of economic and social ills – be they high unemployment, low productivity, declining morals or juvenile delinquency. Labour Prime Minister James Callaghan's *Great Debate* speech at Ruskin College, Oxford, in 1976 marked a significant turning point. Callaghan made specific connections between education and the economy, particularly the perceived inability of schools and colleges to produce young people with the skills, abilities and dispositions needed by employers. Effectively, much of the responsibility for the UK's declining economic performance was placed with the education system. Although such claims had a certain populist appeal, especially to those opposed to the so-called progressive forms of teaching that gained some popularity in the 1960s and 1970s, Callaghan's speech both over-simplified and individualised a phenomenon with complex and deep-rooted causes. The Great Debate paved the way for an approach in which education is expected almost exclusively to provide the UK's route to salvation, despite the lack of convincing evidence for a direct relationship between education and economic success. Issues such as macro-economic policy, the chronic failure of UK employers to invest in up-to-date plant and technology, and endemic management short-termism were all overlooked.

The assumptions of neo-liberalism are significantly different from those of the post-war consensus. For thirty years after the end of the Second World War there was a broad commitment by all the main political parties that the state would help to create employment and promote equality through Keynesian economic policies, a redistributive system of taxation, and the stimulation of employment through a corporatist approach involving government, trade unions and employers as partners in formulating and implementing policy. Alongside a welfare state with free health care, a greatly expanded education system, and the provision of a range of universal benefits, there was a general belief that government could play a positive role in promoting greater equality, and there was substantial agreement between Labour and the Conservatives over central policy issues. This consensus was, however, under considerable strain by the middle of the 1970s. Deep public spending cuts and pay restraint policies introduced as a condition of the IMF loan brought matters to a head, and the Labour Party lost power in the aftermath of widespread industrial unrest.

The election of Mrs Thatcher as Prime Minister in 1979 brought a new *weltanschauung*, and the principles of the post-war consensus were rapidly abandoned. Following two successive general election defeats in 1974, key Conservative figures had sought an alternative to consensus politics and, by the time of its election victory, neo-liberalism was firmly in the ascendancy within the Conservative Party, informed by the ideas of Von Hayek, Friedman and other prominent neo-liberal thinkers. Vehemently opposed to the politics of the post-war consensus, Mrs Thatcher instead favoured individualism and entrepreneurialism. Alongside weakening trade unions, cutting taxation and reducing welfare provision, she was firmly committed to shrinking the public sector, and injecting privatisation and marketisation into all parts of the economy.

Mrs Thatcher's decade in power brought about significant changes in the nature of British society and, although her premiership ended over twenty years ago, its legacy lives on. Successive UK governments – Conservative, New Labour and Coalition – have remained resolutely committed to economic neo-liberalism and a belief in the efficacy of the free-market. Admittedly, there have been some different emphases among the various governments which have been in power since the end of the 1970s; New Labour, for example, placed a stronger emphasis on social inclusion. However, as Avis (2007) argues, all have been committed to securing the conditions under which it is believed capital can best prosper. Consequently, neo-liberalism has strengthened its hegemony and now reaches into virtually all parts of society. For the education system, this has entailed a re-thinking of both problems and solutions: not only must education serve more directly the needs of the economy; educational institutions must themselves operate according to neo-liberal principles, with consumer choice, markets and competition being introduced across all age ranges.

Knowledge, economy and education

Despite different responses to globalisation, one common theme, particularly for nations such as the UK and the USA, has been a growing emphasis upon the importance of the so-called knowledge economy. According to this perspective, nations such as the UK should concentrate on value-added, niche market products and services utilising high skill, specialised labour processes (Avis, 2007). Typically, pharmaceuticals, information technology, bespoke manufacturing, the media and various other creative industries are cited as examples of employment in the knowledge economy. It is widely assumed that human capital – the skills, knowledge and innovative capacities of the workforce – will in future be the most important form of capital for advanced economies.

Some commentators, like the American academic, Gary Becker, go so far as to argue that the USA and the UK, for example, are fast becoming human capital or knowledge capital economies rather than simply capitalist economies. According to Becker, physical and financial capital is becoming less important than the skills, abilities and aptitudes of the workforce. Technology is viewed as the vehicle through which to achieve prosperity but a highly skilled workforce is seen as the fuel which will enable it to run (Becker, 2006:292). Such discourses assume that low-skill and raw material-intensive production will increasingly be located in poorer nations located, for example, in Asia, Latin America and Eastern Europe. Attempting to compete with such economies on the basis of bulk and cost is seen as unviable. For the West, it is thought that the future will prioritise brains over brawn.

Such understandings of the economy and social relations have certain implications for education. Following this logic, there is a need to re-formulate and realign education systems in order to meet the demands of a labour market which will in future be based around high-skill labour processes. In the UK, official discourse claims that if the education system could produce the desired number and mix of skilled workers, individuals, businesses and the nation as a whole would benefit from a new global division of labour. At the same time, however, it is fashionable to criticise education as failing to deliver the skilled workforce necessary for the knowledge economy. It is claimed that this situation – unless reversed – will lead to failure in the global marketplace which will, in turn, lead to social and economic calamity. Over the last twenty years or so this discourse has become pervasive; indeed it appeared almost entirely to shape the education policy of successive New Labour governments. Such assertions were perhaps most clearly articulated in the Leitch Report of 2006. Although aimed specifically at the English FE sector, this report became broadly emblematic of their education policy.

> Our nation's skills are not world class and we run the risk that this will under-
> mine the UK's long-term prosperity ... without increased skills we would
> condemn ourselves to a lingering decline in competitiveness, diminishing
> economic growth and a bleaker future for all. (Leitch, 2006:1)

These and similar claims can be seen as a manifestation of dominant neo-liberal understandings of the knowledge economy and the supposed impact of globalisation. Traditional time-bound forms of work and study are constructed as inadequate, and lifelong learning becomes the key to success. Well before its 1997 election victory, New Labour placed education at the heart of its policies. This, it was claimed, was the best economic strategy for the new global marketplace. Education and training would have an unprecedented role in creating the human capital needed for UK plc to find new markets in the fast-changing global economy. Labour and capital were constructed as having congruent and harmonious interests.

However, de-industrialisation does not necessarily reduce unskilled work, and popular characterisations of the knowledge economy can be rejected for several reasons. One is that such a discourse does not accurately reflect the nature of most forms of work and employment in the UK in general, and in England in particular (Brown *et al*, 2001). The proportion of skilled craft work in the UK has fallen steadily over the past thirty years. In contrast, the fastest growing area of work in the 1980s was in postal delivery; in the 1990s it was the job of care assistant; in the first decade of the new millennium, it was call centre work that experienced huge growth (Wolf, 2002:48-49).

Despite continuing claims about the importance of skills in securing economic success, the UK – and especially England – is trapped in what Finegold and Soskice (1988) famously described as a low-skills equilibrium. The economy relies mainly on low-cost, low-specification and often low-quality goods and services which can be afforded by those on low incomes, either at home or abroad. Although it is possible for different sectors within a particular economy to operate at different equilibrium levels, it is nevertheless possible to distinguish between nations in this way (Iversen, 2005). Atkinson and Elliott (2007:37) argue that high-skills research and development is confined to just two sectors in the UK: pharmaceuticals and aerospace. Both of these indus-

27

tries are heavily subsidised by the state. Work in the UK is in fact polarising, with a minority engaged in the production and distribution of knowledge and a preponderance of employment located in relatively low-skilled and routine labour.

Another problem with the notion of the knowledge economy is that such a label obscures the realities of capitalist relations. It must be noted that, increasingly, trans-national companies are attempting to construct high-value, low-cost models of production in attempting to compete for market share and generate profit. Implicit within the assumption that the West will necessarily reap the rewards of the knowledge economy is the expectation that the poorer nations of the so-called third world will pick up the dirty work. Little consideration is given to the possibility that workers in Asia or Africa may be as able as those in Europe, the USA or elsewhere to carry out advanced labour processes. However, developments in information technology and narrowing differences in productivity increasingly enable not only routine production processes but also various forms of professional and technical work to be carried out in low-wage economies. Consequently, it is likely that cost pressures will intensify upon the workforce in Western Europe and North America (Brown *et al*, 2008). One outcome of this may be further growth of poorly paid work even where high levels of skill are required – not only in the developing world but also in the UK and similar economies.

Neo-liberal discourses construct intervention in labour and product markets as inappropriate and likely to endanger social and economic well-being. Such practices, it is argued, would only hamper the nation's performance in an increasingly global marketplace. According to this *zeitgeist*, skill supply initiatives are seen as one of the few legitimate areas for state intervention (Keep, 2006:58). Consequently, there is an intensive focus upon education and training which is both exaggerated and disproportionate in relation to its contribution to economic competitiveness. Whilst UK business and the labour market are amongst the most lightly regulated in the Western world, it is somewhat ironic that an ideological commitment to the free market has led to its education and training systems becoming amongst the most centrally controlled and directed in the word (Bassey, 2003).

Employability and labour market returns

Contrary to official UK discourse, the relationship between education, employment and labour market returns is not straightforward. It is, however, possible to identify a number of long-term trends related to such matters. One of the most notable is an increasing mismatch between qualification levels and the availability of employment requiring such credentials. Despite great increases in the supply of qualified labour, the anticipated growth of the knowledge economy has not taken place. Despite assertions often made by politicians and business leaders about chronic shortages of appropriately qualified and skilled workers, this is not the case in most areas of employment. In most sectors of the economy the supply of suitable applicants for work is more than ample. One consequence of this is that many young people now find themselves overqualified for most of the opportunities available to them (Ainley and Allen, 2010).

Nowadays policymakers, employers and many educationalists often assert the need to increase levels of employability. However, employability is a slippery notion, and merits further exploration to unpick some of its underpinning assumptions. Some individual qualities and skills, for example, basic literacy and numeracy and the possession of generally acceptable levels of personal awareness, could be seen as necessary for virtually all forms of employment in the twenty-first century (Lindsay, 2002). However, attempts to define employability purely in terms of individual characteristics fail to recognise what Brown *et al* (2003:110) describe as the 'duality of employability'. That is, employability exists in two dimensions: the absolute and the relative. Employability is shaped by economic and labour market conditions as well as the possession of certain individual skills and abilities. In times of labour shortages many unemployed people may become employable; in contrast, when jobs are in short supply, even those with high-level skills, qualifications and extensive experience may find themselves without a job. The notion of employability is further complicated by issues of social identity and societal expectations. In addition to the availability of work and individual attributes, a person's relative chance of obtaining various kinds of employment can be influenced by their social class, gender and ethnic group membership (Simmons, 2009:143).

Official discourse on employability attempts to redefine and individualise the employment relationship. The notion of employability can also been seen as a way of attempting to justify or even glamourise the increasingly insecure nature of work and employment. Whereas previous generations generally enjoyed greater continuity of employment, dominant discourse describes the end of so-called jobs for life and the need to be flexible and adaptable in a rapidly changing labour market.

A positive spin is sometimes attached to such insecurity: whereas the worker is seen to be in a dependent state in traditional forms of employment, contemporary discourses of employability encourage the individual to be more independent and open minded about the world of work. Individuals are required to be creative and to manage their own employability (Tomlinson, 2007:288). Either way, the worker is expected to develop the capabilities deemed necessary to obtain and retain employment (Hillage and Pollard, 1998:1).

Whilst the demand for employment is taken for granted, economic risk is individualised and workers are required to adapt to new economic realities (Brown, Green and Lauder, 2001). Whilst governments argue that job creation is no longer the responsibility of the state, the focus has shifted to promoting individual employability and exhorting the workforce to develop the necessary skills and abilities to be able to adapt to new economic realities. Both individual and national prosperity supposedly rest upon our ability to embrace such a future (Brown and Hesketh, 2004:20-22).

Various other factors influence the employability of young people. Not least of these is the disappearance of a distinct youth labour market that is qualitatively different from employment experienced by other workers, and MacDonald *et al* (2005) point towards a secondary labour market encompassing the economically marginalised of all ages. This market, it is argued, is characterised by pervasive unemployment and chronically insecure, poor quality work. Many of the difficulties encountered by young people can therefore be seen as part of a wider working-class experience, rather than as instances of social exclusion applying only to a residue of ill-prepared youth. Despite this, attempts to stimulate the demand for skilled labour have been largely abandoned (Keep, 2006).

The relative position of most workers has deteriorated in terms of pay and job security but young people tend to be more vulnerable than other workers to the vicissitudes of the labour market. In times of recession, employers are less likely to hire young workers, and they are also more likely to be laid off because they cost less in terms of redundancy payments. Those young people employed in jobs without training are at highest risk of unemployment (Corney, 2009).

The vulnerability of young people in the labour market is illustrated by recent research conducted by the Joseph Rowntree Foundation: by mid-2010, the unemployment rate among 16 to 24-year-olds was, at 20 per cent, three times higher than the rate for other workers. In contrast, after the recession of the early 1990s the rate of unemployment for the same category of young people was 16 per cent – roughly twice as high as for the rest of the population (Parekh *et al*, 2010:1). This is despite significant improvements in educational attainment. The number of pupils not gaining five GCSEs fell by one-third between 2004 and 2009. Over the same period, the number of 19-year-olds without at least an NVQ level 2 or equivalent qualification fell from 28 to 23 per cent. Interestingly, the last government had set the educational benchmark of employability as the achievement of a level 2 qualification (Simmons, 2009:143). At the other end of the spectrum, by 2011, graduate unemployment had reached a 10 year high. One in five recent graduates was unable to find work (UCU, 2011).

Individualisation, risk and the state

Neo-liberalism contains a number of assumptions about the nature of people and the role of the state. It starts by proposing that there are innate differences between individuals: for example, in terms of intelligence, motivation and moral character. Furthermore, people are seen, ultimately, as self-interested. Individuals, it is claimed, function best and are able to contribute most effectively – both to their own welfare and to the economy in general – when they are allowed to follow their private interests.

As it is believed that hierarchies based upon ability will naturally and inevitably emerge, attempts to reduce inequalities are assumed to be flawed. Rather than redistributing wealth, neo-liberalism proposes that the state should encourage and motivate the disadvantaged to stand on

31

their own two feet. Self-reliance is promoted and individual rather than collective responses are seen as the best way of overcoming uncertainties in the labour market (Brown *et al*, 2001; Lauder *et al*, 2006:25). Guaranteed employment would, in any case, only make the workforce complacent and uncompetitive and industry inefficient. Young people in particular are encouraged to develop their human capital, and acquire the flexible, compliant dispositions deemed attractive to employers. Workers are required to train and retrain themselves on an ongoing basis in order to keep up with the changing and intensifying demands of employment. The individual must take responsibility for creating and maintaining themselves as socially and economically useful agents if they are to avoid social exclusion.

Neo-liberal governments do more than exhort individuals to develop and maintain employability; they also focus on dismantling perceived barriers to participation in education, training and the labour market. Collective bargaining and other so-called restrictive practices, such as trade union involvement in apprenticeship schemes, are viewed as particularly negative. Such arrangements, it is argued, can only impede the natural order of the market, drive up costs and, in turn, create unemployment.

Traditional forms of managing and delivering education and training are also seen as deeply problematic. Public sector provision, especially if run by local authorities, is constructed as bureaucratic and ineffective, as well as unresponsive to the needs of business. Consequently, the state needs to intervene to tackle the forces of conservativism and inertia. Restrictive practices need to be tackled and public services freed from vested interests. Education systems, it is argued, need to be dynamic and responsive to meet the customer needs of individuals, business and other clients. If it is not possible to privatise provision directly then service providers need to be compelled to behave like businesses operating in a competitive marketplace.

Although broadly constituting a single political era, there were differences in style and emphasis between the Conservative governments of Thatcher and Major, and their New Labour successors. The priority given to tackling social exclusion through education and training is one example. However, whilst New Labour discourse prioritised such matters, in reality it accepted, and in some cases extended, many of the neo-liberal principles that became dominant under Thatcherism (Hodgson and Spours, 2006; Byrne, 2005).

This can be seen both in macro-economic policy and in particular initiatives relating to the role and purpose of education. Whilst New Labour assumed uncritically, and perhaps somewhat naively, that the interests of labour and capital would naturally and inevitably coincide, there was an increased commercialisation of state provision, and private and voluntary sector providers were actively encouraged to enter the educational marketplace. Meanwhile, teachers, lecturers and other education workers were subject to increasingly stringent mechanisms of audit, accountability, inspection and control. More broadly, the Labour Party's shift away from a redistributive approach towards welfare to one based upon inclusion and employability demonstrated a decisive break with its social democratic past. Ultimately, the individual rather than the state would be responsible for managing his or her own well-being.

Social exclusion in the UK

Although policymakers and academics in the UK have traditionally talked in terms of poverty and the condition of the poor, the term 'social exclusion' has more continental roots and stems chiefly from European Christian democratic politics. Contemporary debates and discussions about social exclusion entered academia from the domain of political discourse, and since the mid-1990s social exclusion has become an increasingly common term in the UK, often associated with New Labour and so-called Third Way politics (Byrne, 2005:52-53). The priority placed upon tackling social exclusion can be linked with attempts to mediate between the conflict and inequality generated by free market capitalism and the desire to maintain and legitimate an inclusive social order.

However, the term social exclusion is itself open to some interpretation and there are different understandings of the term. Ruth Levitas (2005) offers a useful framework which helps us to understand such matters. She identifies three discourses of social exclusion, each with a different emphasis and different consequences: a traditional redistributive discourse; a discourse of social integration; and a moralistic discourse based on notions of underclass and dependency.

33

Varying discourses of exclusion can be associated with different political regimes. The redistributionist version of social exclusion can be equated with traditional Labour Party social policy, or at least with the centre-right of the Party which was particularly influential during the 1960s and 1970s. Underlying this approach is the desire to redistribute wealth through progressive taxation, and increase equality by providing a broad range of public services, comprehensive benefits and welfare systems. In contrast, the social integrationist discourse is rooted in German order-liberalism and in its UK variant, emphasises the importance of employment and the role of paid work in promoting social inclusion and an integrated, cohesive society. The third strand identified by Levitas is the discourse of a moral underclass. This discourse can be seen as part of a particular Thatcherite strand of neo-liberalism; in academia it is perhaps most often associated with the work of the right-wing American sociologist, Charles Murray (1990; 1994).

Whilst the politics of redistribution are linked chiefly with the post-war consensus, Levitas saw New Labour policies on social exclusion as increasingly shaped by a combination of the two latter discourses. By employing this combination of approaches, New Labour was able to distance itself to some degree from the politics of Thatcherism, which were often seen as harsh and authoritarian, whilst maintaining a broad commitment to neo-liberalism, a stance deemed necessary because of the pressures of globalisation and the associated need to abandon traditional social democratic values.

Several trends were associated with this. One was a shift away from class-based politics or indeed any meaningful engagement with social class as a concept based in structural inequality. Alongside this, attempts to tackle the inherent conflicts of interest between labour and capital were abandoned. In place of serious efforts to redistribute wealth was a much more individualised approach to social exclusion. New Labour concentrated mainly on developing various policies and initiatives which attempted to integrate the poor back into society through changing their attitudes, dispositions and habits.

Whilst some of its initiatives were not without value and some, such as Sure Start, made a real difference in deprived neighbourhoods, much of New Labour's social politics can be traced back to largely individualistic understandings of social exclusion, whether it was the drive to widen participation in education and training, or the attempt to promote better public health through healthy eating and anti-smoking campaigns.

In the UK, politicians from any of the main political parties rarely mention, let alone prioritise issues of social class any more. In academia the fashion for postmodernism that took root in some circles, particularly from the 1980s onwards, led to less emphasis upon class as an analytical tool, and more interest in other forms of identity and difference. In some ways this is understandable: the UK is now a multicultural society; many traditional working-class institutions, such as trade unions, working men's clubs, and the Labour Party are less central to the lives of many ordinary people than was the case in previous decades.

Clearly, conceptions of social class have altered notably over the last thirty years or more. But whilst many no longer readily identify with membership of the working-class, this does not necessarily mean that class has become irrelevant. Although the traditional pyramid model of social class that existed in the post-war era may well be outdated, there are still significant class-based divisions in the UK in the twenty-first century. The notion that expanded white-collar and service sector employment has somehow transformed the class structure and that the majority of people are now essentially middle class seems inaccurate, as well as overly optimistic. The growth in white-collar employment has masked the realities of most people's working lives. Most of those who could be identified as lower middle class according to various occupational scales earn relatively less than would have been the case had they been in skilled working-class employment a generation ago (Lansley, 2009:10).

Nowadays almost one third of all jobs in the UK are low paid, paying less than two thirds of the median wage (Keep, 2009). Meanwhile, the income of those in the top echelons of society has grown massively. Consequently, social class in the UK today could be illustrated by a long-waisted hour-glass. Patrick Ainley and Martin Allen go still further. Describing an ideologically and politically constructed underclass of unemployed and under-employed individuals, where large sections of the old working-class have become relegated to a life of insecure, transitory employment interspersed with periods of unemployment and other forms of economic inactivity, they see the UK's class structure as developing increasingly into a pear shape (Allen and Ainley, 2007:32-34).

Ethnicity can be another dimension of social exclusion. There is some evidence of ethnic segregation in the UK, for example the high concentration of Bangladeshis in the East End of London and of Pakistanis in parts of Bradford and certain other areas of West Yorkshire and East Lancashire. Racial hostility has meant that people of South Asian origin have traditionally been less likely to live in local authority housing. There is, however, little evidence of such discrimination in middle-class areas. Somewhat paradoxically, ethnic exclusion in the UK has tended to feature exclusion mainly from certain less desirable locales.

In contrast to the USA, the main dimension of spatial exclusion in the UK is not race, but social class (Byrne, 2005:121-122). This is not a new phenomenon – Engels (1892) recognised the separateness of the different social classes in nineteenth century Manchester. Over time, such divisions reduced and were ameliorated by the reductions in inequality that characterised the social democratic consensus of the mid-twentieth century. However, in the last thirty years there have been significant increases in spatial segregation, especially class-based divisions in housing. According to Wacquant (1999) these increases are associated with the stigmatisation of poverty, casualisation of labour, retrenchment of the welfare state, and higher levels of inequality in general.

Spatial exclusion is perhaps the most visible form of social exclusion, its effects being particularly important as they involve differential access to public services such as health care, and especially schooling. This, in turn, affects future life chances, including opportunities for further education and employment (Byrne, 2005:117). However, whilst space, especially in urban areas, is becoming polarised according to social class, social relations are becoming less coherent and more atomised. Traditional working-class identities have been fractured by macro-economic forces, de-industrialisation and individualistic self-interest promoted by the politics of neo-liberalism (Wilson, 1992). A number of studies of deprived towns and cities in UK, the USA and Europe have highlighted the consequences of such processes, which Byrne (1995: 127) describes as promoting a culture of disablement.

Widening participation

In the UK, far greater numbers of people participate in post-compulsory education and training than in previous decades. There are two main ways in which this has been achieved: by including more people from groups already well represented, and through widening participation from traditionally under-represented sections of society. Although some of this increase in participation can be explained by the increased availability of white-collar work, especially in the public sector, it is doubtful whether much of the increased rate of educational participation can be described as an active choice by those concerned. As much of the traditional youth labour market has disappeared, or since such jobs are increasingly taken by older and sometimes more highly qualified workers, it is perhaps unsurprising that most young people now continue their education, often for many years, after the minimum school leaving age.

Although substantially increased levels of participation, especially since the 1980s, are associated with limited alternatives for many young people, the benefits of greater access to education must also be recognised. Not least of these is the relatively improved position of girls and women. Whilst gender equality still varies significantly between different social and ethnic groups in the UK, there is little doubt that women have in general benefited from widening participation. Although discrimination based upon gender, race or any other form of difference has not been eradicated from society, some of the grosser forms of bias and discrimination that formerly characterised both education and the workplace are generally no longer socially acceptable. As well as broader changes in social norms and expectations, this shift can be linked, at least in part, to increases in educational participation, especially by females.

Increased participation in post-compulsory education is partly a rational, almost organic reaction to broader structural changes in society. Nevertheless, it is important to understand the role of the state in this process. Whilst presiding over far-reaching changes in the economy and labour markets, successive governments have actively encouraged increased participation in education and training. A range of motives underpin this, but it is possible to identify at least three strands of sometimes inter-related thinking on this matter. One of these has already been discussed and relates to notions of economic competitiveness based upon human capital theory. Another is rooted in the state's desire to maintain and increase social control. Finally, in the case of New Labour at least, there was also a genuine, if not coherent or critical wish to promote social inclusion. It is to these two latter motives that this section will now turn.

Much contemporary discourse promotes education as an empowering and positive experience for all. However, this was not always the case. In the late eighteenth century, Adam Smith described the role of education in controlling the lower orders:

> An instructed and intelligent people besides are always more decent and orderly than an ignorant one ... less apt to be misled into any wanton or unnecessary opposition to the measures of the government. (Smith, 1785:305)

It is unlikely that policymakers in the twenty-first century would express such sentiments quite so vividly. Nevertheless, it is important to note that, whilst increased levels of educational participation have been promoted across society, notably different forms of participation are apparent for different social groups. Furthermore, different groups of people are encouraged to participate in education and training for different reasons. With the breakdown of traditional youth transitions, especially for working-class young people, educational institutions have an increasingly important role to play in maintaining social order (Allen and Ainley, 2007:34). The declining importance of work as a source of income and identity for large sections of the working-class has positioned the extension of schooling and various forms of education and training as an important regulating force. This function is especially transparent in the case of the unemployed and other groups classified as economically inactive. Many welfare benefits are now conditional upon engaging in training programmes supposedly linked to increasing the employability of recipients.

Historically, the English education system was quite overt in its discrimination against those from working-class backgrounds. Even after the state became involved in providing universal education, for the majority of working-class children this did not extend beyond elementary school. It was not until the 1944 Education Act that free secondary schooling was made available to all. However, despite the post-war spirit of social reconstruction and a broad commitment to increasing equality across society, the new tripartite system of grammar, technical and secondary modern schools introduced in the years after the end of World War Two allowed systematic class-based divisions to continue, only this time it was justified upon the basis of so-called scientific testing rather than upon the ability to pay. Under the tripartite system, pupils deemed to possess certain aptitudes and abilities were assigned to grammar, technical or secondary modern schools based upon performance in a national examination known as the 11-plus. Under this regime, a pupil's educational future and, in turn, working life depended largely upon a psychometric test promoted as a fair and objective measurement of individual intelligence.

The divisive system of selection which underpinned the tripartite system was justified not only on the basis of supposed innate differences in ability between pupils but also on the perceived needs of business and industry for different grades of workers with varying skills and ambitions. However, the 11-plus was culturally biased against working-class children, as well as systematically loaded against girls who had to achieve a higher mark to pass the examination. Consequently, the tripartite system helped to perpetuate and justify discrimination on the basis of social class and gender that has always been present in the English education system. Furthermore, the 1944 Education Act failed to tackle one of the most overt and deeply-rooted forms of inequality in the education system – the thorny issue of fee-paying schools. These exclusive institutions serving the most privileged sections of society were effectively left exempt from state control. Indeed, they have been allowed to exist virtually untouched ever since (Allen and Ainley, 2007: 16-18).

The shift towards comprehensive schooling from the 1960s onwards went some way towards ameliorating the bias and discrimination inherent within the tripartite system. However, comprehensives were never universally adopted across England; some local authorities refused to abandon their grammar schools and, from the 1980s onwards, successive governments have actively undermined the comprehensive movement. Whether this has been through the Conservative reforms of the 1980s and 1990s, via New Labour's drive for increased diversity and choice, or the current Coalition Government's intensification of their predecessor's approach through the promotion of Academies and the attempt to introduce so-called Free Schools, a series of policy initiatives have increasingly fractured and splintered schooling according to religious, ethnic and especially class-based divisions. As a result, the English education system is today perhaps more differentiated and un-equal than at any time since World War Two.

Somewhat paradoxically, the overall rise in qualification levels and the great increase in participation in post-compulsory education appear, in some ways, to have contributed to inequality. On one level this is quite straightforward to understand. As the gap grows between those with few or no qualifications and the increasingly certificated mass, this divide becomes more and more difficult to bridge for those at the bottom. As the supply of qualified labour continues to grow, employers can afford to be increasingly selective in their recruitment and retention strategies. Those without the desired credentials become more likely to be cut adrift from the mainstream labour market and more vulnerable to unemployment, underemployment and poor employment. Recent research conducted on behalf of the Joseph Rowntree Foundation shows the existence of a low-pay, no-pay cycle for many working-class people. It highlights a significant casualisation of the labour market, especially at the lower end, with a pattern of repeated churning be-tween low-paid, low-skilled, short-term jobs, benefit dependency and unemployment (Shildrick *et al*, 2010). In a highly competitive labour market, those outside the credentialised norm are particularly vulner-able to low pay, insecurity and recurrent poverty.

On another level, for those engaged in education and training, different groups of young people undertake an experience sharply differentiated by social class as well as by gender and ethnicity. At one end, fee-paying schools, the more prestigious state school sixth-forms and sixth-form colleges continue to provide predominantly high status academic courses such as A-levels, although some also offer other courses per-ceived to be of high status, such as the International Baccalaureate. Those in the middle are directed towards various vocational and applied qualifications. More often than not, low level qualifications based upon fashionable notions of employability and vocational preparation are aimed at the disaffected, the resistant and other variously more challenging sections of young people in society. It is this category of learner for whom programmes such as E2E are designed and targeted. Such patterns of participation make it possible to discern new forms of tripartism developing, where different forms of engagement are intended for different categories of young people (Allen and Ainley, 2007:96-97).

Work, training and welfare

Although training and workforce skills – especially in relation to rising international competition – had been seen as an important political issue for some time beforehand, it is possible to trace a marked change in policy towards these issues from the end of the post-war consensus. This involved a shift away from the corporatist approach to employment and training that had characterised this era. In its place increasingly individualised approaches to employability, with a focus on supply-side initiatives as supposed solutions to perceived skill and labour shortages have been promoted. The first of these was the Youth Opportunities Programme (YOP), introduced in 1978 to offer work experience, training and work preparation for the growing number of school leavers unable to find employment as the decline of the UK's traditional industrial base accelerated in the aftermath of the oil crisis of the early 1970s. From this point, one can trace some of the assumptions that came to shape E2E and other programmes aimed at increasing the employability of disengaged young people.

Although there have been some differences in emphasis between the various programmes introduced, Tusting and Barton (2007) argue that a lineage can be traced through the numerous vocational training programmes introduced by the Conservative governments of Margaret Thatcher and John Major, right up to those which are offered in the twenty-first century. Be they the Youth Training Schemes (YTS) or Youth Training (YT) courses of the 1980s and 1990s, the various New Deal programmes created by New Labour, or any of the multitude of vocational training programmes introduced over the last three decades, certain continuities remain. The underlying assumptions of such provision adopt a deficit model in the way they approach the employability of adults and young people. All assume that the causes of high levels of unemployment lie primarily in the shortcomings of individuals and the ineffectiveness of mainstream educational provision to equip them with the skills and abilities they require to become employable. Alternative causes of unemployment such as a lack of job opportunities, low levels of demand for skill, or economic policy tend to be ignored.

The issue of employability has not always been viewed in such a narrow and individualistic fashion. Somewhat ironically, the organisation responsible for introducing YOP and numerous similar schemes, the Manpower Services Commission (MSC), was originally conceived to work with employers and trade unions to promote increased levels of demand for skills, as well as to increase skill supply. Its ambitious goals also included elevating the importance of vocational learning, and redefining its contribution to national development (Ainley and Corney, 1990:2). However, the MSC's original mission was blown off course and such ambitions were never realised. Forced to focus on fire-fighting measures to tackle growing youth unemployment, by the late 1970s the MSC had effectively become focused on work substitution. One notable characteristic of the Commission was that, despite its origins as a corporatist body, it effectively pioneered the introduction of market forces in post-compulsory education and training in England.

Although many FE colleges were involved in YOP and similar schemes, they were funded by the Department of Employment directly rather than via local authorities. The Commission also led the way in using private and voluntary providers to deliver state funded training programmes. Such an approach can be seen as an early example of what has sometimes been described as the contracting state – a situation where, rather than providing services directly, the state enters into commercial contracts with third parties to carry out work on its behalf. Similar practices are now commonplace in the delivery of work-based learning programmes across the country. Such arrangements illustrate what can be described as a new mixed economy of public service provision in the UK, whereby traditional divisions between public and private sectors increasingly break down and blur (Allen and Ainley, 2007:72). Under this system, state-subsidised private companies and semi-privatised public sector providers intermingle and compete with each other for business in government-led markets. This trend is discernable not only in education and training but in many other areas of public service provision; for example, in delivering social services, health care and what is now often described as social housing.

New Deal, introduced in 1998 by Tony Blair's first New Labour Government and which operated until its abolition by the Coalition Government in autumn 2010, provides a clear example of both individualised notions of employability and the commercialisation of training provision expected to re-moralise and equip the workless to secure employment. Originally conceived for those aged 18-24, New Deal soon expanded and multiplied to encompass various programmes for older unemployed people, as well as provision targeted at specific groups deemed worthy of special attention. New Deal for Young People (NDYP) was, however, by far the largest of these programmes and contained a number of features that Peck (2001) describes as characterising a system of *workfare*.

One of the features of NDYP was mandatory participation. Continued receipt of benefits was dependent upon taking part in the programme. Underpinning this approach is the principle that nobody should expect unconditional or ongoing social welfare. It is assumed, instead, that the low end of the labour market should become the main means of support for the socially excluded, although the state is prepared to subsidise employers who offered low-paid work, through using welfare payments such as the Working Families Tax Credit to supplement rates of pay that would otherwise fail to provide a living wage. Byrne (2005:111) compares this arrangement to the Speenhamland system established in eighteenth century England, which encouraged and perpetuated low-paid work.

Although New Deal was state funded, much of the training provided was supplied by either private companies or voluntary sector organisations. As such, it combined an ongoing commitment to the entrepreneurial values of neo-liberalism and a faith in the market to deliver public services with processes of correction and discipline for those seen to be work shy. Although New Deal is now effectively defunct, it is unlikely that there will be any significant shift in approach towards training and its relationship to benefits in the foreseeable future. The Coalition Government has pledged to launch a replacement for New Deal. Due to be launched in summer 2011, the Single Work Programme will encompass all those without work, regardless of the cause of their unemployment or the benefit they receive (Island Pulse, 2010), and is intended to increase the involvement of private and voluntary sector organisations in providing routes back into work for the unemployed (Baker, 2010).

Welfare benefits for the poor are increasingly conditional on under-taking work or training. Meanwhile, employers benefit substantially from an increased pool of labour, as well as state subsidies which enable wage bills to be held down. Such practices are not, however, confined to employers operating in low pay, low skill sectors of the economy. Tradi-tionally, one reason why young people from working-class backgrounds have been less likely to enter prestigious professions such as medicine, architecture or law has been the extended courses of study and often un-paid or poorly paid periods of work experience required to become a fully qualified practitioner. Furthermore, the growing culture of intern-ships is likely to exclude still more young people from an ever wider range of graduate-level work than has been the case hitherto. This, in turn, is likely to contribute to further polarisation of the labour market. Unable to sacrifice pay or afford the accommodation, travel and subsis-tence costs required to undertake an internship, the barriers facing those from working-class backgrounds are formidable.

3
Sixty Years of Youth Transitions

This chapter conceptualises the changing nature of youth transitions over the past 60 years, which have altered considerably. We discuss the position of young people in post-war England, and traditional approaches to understanding their transitions from school to work. We identify the ways in which the experiences of young people have become more complex and often turbulent, focusing particularly on changes in work, education and employment in recent decades. We explain how these changes have led to the term *transition* being regarded by some as outmoded and inappropriate; and how alternative conceptions have challenged established ways of understanding the life experience of young people. The chapter concludes by focusing on the experiences of young people in the early twenty-first century. Whilst objective and subjective changes have affected the lives of all young people, we argue that their impact is differentiated according to gender, race and, in particular, social class. New subjectivities and patterns of consumption may seem to provide greater opportunities for young people to create distinctive biographies but for many, their transitions to adulthood are shaped more than ever by structured inequality.

Youth transitions in the post-war era

The years between the end of World War Two and the close of the 1960s are often described as the golden years of British capitalism (eg Hobsbawm, 1995:257). The period was characterised by relatively low levels of unemployment, decreasing levels of inequality, and sustained economic growth. Although competition from overseas gathered pace during the 1950s and 1960s, the UK's established industrial base helped to provide sufficient employment opportunities for most of those seeking work. Meanwhile, post-war reconstruction and the creation of the welfare state greatly expanded health, education and other public services. As well as helping to improve social conditions in general, this greatly increased opportunities for social mobility as new jobs were created in the public sector, especially for professional and white collar workers.

Nonetheless, the majority of young people finished school at the minimum leaving age of 15 (16 from 1973); relatively few entered post-compulsory education; and, even after the expansion of higher education in the 1960s, only around 8 per cent of young people went to university, the majority of whom were white, male and middle class (Harman, 2006). Lengthy periods of study and progression to university were alien concepts to most working-class young people. Until the early 1970s, around 40 per cent of young people left school without any qualifications at all, a proportion not viewed at the time as particularly problematic. Although some pockets of unemployment persisted in the UK, for example, in Northern Ireland, on Merseyside and in parts of Scotland, most young people were able to gain employment consistent with their ambitions and expectations. Many were only too eager to leave education behind and enter the world of work (Willis, 1977).

The most sought-after form of employment for working-class boys was perhaps an apprenticeship. At its high point at the end of the 1960s, a quarter of young workers (mainly males) were engaged in apprenticeships (FECRDU, 1978:34-35). Day-release attendance at a local technical college was often associated with apprenticeship programmes as well as with the growing number of technical and clerical jobs being taken by young people. The majority, however, saw further study after leaving school as superfluous, because unskilled or semi-skilled jobs were generally in plentiful supply. Moreover, young people occupied a relatively privileged position in the labour market; whilst unemployment levels were generally low, youth unemployment tended to be lower than for the general population. Readily available work, increasing levels of prosperity and relatively affordable housing acted in synergy to facilitate rapid youth transitions. The passage from youth to adulthood is generally considered to have been at its most condensed, coherent and unitary during the 1950s and 1960s (Jones, 1995:23). Finishing school and obtaining a job was usually followed fairly rapidly by leaving home, marriage and parenthood. At the beginning of the 1970s, the average age for first marriage was 20 for women and 22 for men, compared with 28 and 30 for women and men respectively forty years later (Ainley and Allen, 2010:21).

For young men especially, transition from school to work was often collective as well as speedy: the movement, en masse, of boys from school into local industry was commonplace. Collective transitions offered a number of attractions. Not least of these were the relatively high wages which were often paid even to those engaged in routine forms of labour. More broadly, the experience of working alongside peers and siblings in the factories, mines and mills that once dominated the UK economy offered certain forms of camaraderie, as well as a climate of stability and continuity. Consequently, it is tempting to look back at the post-war era with a certain fondness.

It would be a mistake, however, to romanticise or over-simplify matters. Hugh Beynon's classic study, *Working for Ford* (Beynon, 1973), revealed some harsh realities of industrial labour in post-war England – an experience that was often bleak, dull and boring, and sometimes acrimonious. The often negative experiences of young people at work are too easily overlooked. Apprenticeships, for example, were based not only on skill acquisition but also on time-serving and socialisation into particular forms of workplace culture. It should not be forgotten that rituals of humiliation, bullying and abuse sometimes accompanied this, especially for young people entering engineering, construction and other areas of employment traditionally associated with particular forms of masculinity.

Whilst class consciousness and solidarity are often associated with traditional proletarian forms of employment, various forms of prejudice and parochialism were not uncommon. Girls and women suffered from systematic and overt discrimination, both in the education system and in the workplace. Other forms of prejudice, including those based on race and religion, were also commonplace, whether in the shipyards of Glasgow and Belfast, the mines and mills of Yorkshire and Lancashire, or the engineering workshops of the English midlands. Furthermore, the uneasy passage of some young people into work and adulthood was hidden by low headline levels of unemployment. Whilst work was generally fairly easy to obtain in post-war England, the notion that young people entered employment and enjoyed the security of a job-for-life is overstated. Many did not settle easily into working life. The chronic job-changing of some young people was masked by the relative availability of work (Finn, 1987:47).

Dennis, Henriques and Slaughter's (1956) study of a West Yorkshire mining community and Young and Wilmott's (1962) research in the docklands of London's East End offer vivid insights into the sometimes harsh realities of working-class life in post-war England. Over the past thirty years such close-knit working-class communities, typically clustered around particular forms of work and employment, have been fragmented and radically altered by the collapse of the UK's traditional industrial base. Some localities have coped with change better than others, but the effects of de-industrialisation have probably been felt most sharply in those working-class communities which traditionally relied upon a single industry for their main source of employment.

Revisiting former mining villages in the late 1990s, Royce Turner (2000) describes a culture and environment soured by demoralisation and disempowerment, and beset by crime, vandalism and drug abuse. Despite various attempts at community regeneration, the demise of the coal industry has had serious effects, particularly for young people in such locales. The scenario described by Turner is one of loss and pain which should not be underestimated. However, nostalgia for the various forms of conservatism and oppression that sometimes also characterised life in the industrial communities of post-war England would be misplaced. Security and solidarity were often accompanied by repression, intolerance and narrow horizons.

Crisis, change and shifting transitions

For most young people, youth transitions have changed radically since the early 1970s. Generally young people now have longer periods of dependency upon their parents; they tend to stay in education, especially on a full-time basis, for longer periods than was the case in previous generations; and they usually enter the labour market at a later age than in the post-war era. This is particularly the case where full-

48

time employment is concerned. What are sometimes described as extended or delayed transitions have been accompanied by later access to the traditional signifiers of adult status. There are similar trends towards delayed adulthood elsewhere: see, for example, the work of Coté and Bynner on Canada (2008); Roberts (2009b) on Eastern Europe and the commentary of Keeley *et al* (2008) on the position of young adults in various countries in Western Europe. Although youth transitions in the UK were once quite distinctive, they now resemble those found in the USA and other parts of Europe (Shildrick and MacDonald, 2007:590-591).

By the end of the 1970s, mass unemployment was commonplace in many parts of the country, especially amongst young people (Tusting and Barton, 2007:12). As the youth labour market rapidly declined, various government-supported training schemes were created in order to deal with the growing number of unemployed young people. Such was the growth of youth unemployment that YOP and similar MSC-run schemes soon became the most likely destination for the majority of school leavers, and by 1983 over three million young people were enrolled on youth training programmes. YOP and its successors such as YTS were often criticised as poor quality and, in some cases, employers abused such provision, using young people as cheap labour and providing little meaningful training or work experience in return.

It must be noted, however, that not all such programmes were exploitative. A broad range of employers were involved, including blue chip and market-leading organisations. Many took the development of young people seriously, providing them with extensive workplace training, and generous time off to attend college in addition to the minimum allowance paid by the state. Often, such employers would offer permanent employment at the end of training placements.

Either way, the experiences of many young people on youth training programmes led to a negative image of such provision. Many chose to avoid them altogether and, by the mid-1980s, more than half of all 16 and 17-year-olds and a quarter of all 18 and 19 year olds were unemployed (Finn, 1987:187; Mizen, 2004:55).

MSC training provision became a way of disguising and managing youth unemployment. Some went so far as to describe the MSC as the

Ministry of Social Control (Allen and Ainley, 2007). Such schemes also depressed wages, particularly for young people. Increasingly, young people chose to stay on at school to avoid the daunting options facing them: unemployment, disqualification from most benefits, and generally poor vocational training. Lack of employment opportunities combined with the failure of vocational training led many young people to turn to mainstream education. From the late 1980s onwards there were huge increases in young people staying on at school or entering further education. In many ways this can be seen as a pragmatic decision caused by a lack of other viable options. Whilst Finn (1987) described the 1980s as a period of *training without jobs*, Ainley and Allen (2010) have described the period that followed it as *education without jobs*.

School to work in the 21st century

Despite the existence of a significant number of NEET young people, some 87 per cent of school leavers in England now go on to some form of education and training immediately after the end of compulsory education, and over 75 per cent are still participating two years after the minimum leaving age of 16 (DfES, 2007:9-10). In theory at least, this is voluntary. Their participation does, however, need to be seen within the context of the severe curtailment of full-time employment opportunities for school leavers that has prevailed since the 1970s. Having said this, participation in post-compulsory education and training is lower in the UK than is the case in most comparable societies. Twenty-two of the 30 members of the Organisation for Economic Co-operation and Development (OECD) have higher rates of post-16 participation than the UK. This includes not only many other northern European nations, but also countries to which the UK would traditionally regard itself as socially and economically superior. East European nations such as Poland, Hungary and the Czech Republic, for example, all have higher post-16 participation rates than the UK (DfES, 2007:16-17).

By 2013, participation in some form of education or training will become compulsory for all young people in England up to the age of 17 and, by 2015, the compulsory age of participation will rise to 18. Although these changes are significant, they do not constitute a raising of the school leaving age *per se*. Different forms of participation will be possible and, as long as there is some engagement in education or training, a range of full-time or part-time options will be possible. Sixteen-year-olds will still be able to work full-time as long as they take part in some kind of recognised education or training, whether this takes place with a voluntary, private or public sector provider. Alternatively, they will be required to undertake some form of recognised training as part of their employment.

Such proposals are far from revolutionary. As relatively few young people do not go on to further study after reaching the age of 16, current proposals to raise the minimum age of participation will affect far fewer than previous attempts. Similar proposals to raise the age of participation to 18 were made by the 1918 Fisher Education Act and the 1944 Butler Education Act. For various reasons, including the opposition of some parents to the prospect of their children losing earnings, these plans went largely unfulfilled. Had either initiative come to fruition, their effects would have been far more profound than current proposals. By contrast, other than the small number of 16 to 18-year-olds employed in jobs without training, those likely to be most affected by the current attempt to raise the age of participation are NEET young people (Simmons, 2008).

For most young people, earning a living wage, leaving home, marriage and parenthood all tend to take place at a later age than was the case for their parents, and certainly for their grand-parents. However, it is an over-simplification to describe youth transitions as delayed or extended. In many cases, the traditional and expected sequence of key life events has also been disturbed. Employment, marriage and parenthood, for example, often take place in random order. Sometimes they are suspended almost indefinitely. As a consequence of these and other broad social and cultural changes, traditional ways of conceptualising youth transitions have been subject to sustained criticism. Sometimes they are described as fractured or broken, and alternative ways of understanding the lives of young people are often preferred. Terms such as trajectories, pathways, routes, journeys and navigations are favoured by some commentators. Some suggest a greater degree of agency than others, but all such terms imply that traditional conceptions of youth transitions are inadequate in explaining the life experiences of young people (Shildrick and MacDonald, 2007:590-591). Either way, transitions to adulthood and into work have become increasingly diverse.

> The post-Fordist labour market has not only worked to delay and interrupt traditional youth transition, but it has also worked to complexify them. Young people today make a bewildering array of labour market transitions, including moving through various training and educational routes through to temporary, contract and part-time work, and in some cases to secure employment. (Chatterton and Hollands, 2003:81)

Clearly, the objective circumstances in which young people now find themselves have changed. Since the 1970s there has been the virtual collapse of the traditional youth labour market and the demise of the traditional system of apprenticeships. This has been accompanied by the introduction and growth of training programmes focused, at least officially, on preparing young people for work: significantly increased levels of participation in further and higher education; and welfare changes that have greatly reduced young people's entitlement to benefits. Such changes have been played out against a backdrop of persistent structural unemployment (Shildrick and MacDonald, 2007: 590).

By early 2011, unemployment amongst 16 to 24-year-olds in the UK had reached record levels, with 20 per cent of all young people in this age group without work (BBC, 2011). Youth unemployment is a serious issue elsewhere: in 2010, 25 per cent of young people in France and Italy were unemployed, whereas the rate in Spain was 40 per cent (Scarpetta *et al*, 2010). The OECD reports a significant rise in youth unemployment across all its member nations since the global financial crisis of 2008, and has predicted that unemployment levels amongst young people will continue to rise for the foreseeable future (OECD, 2010). Focusing on headline rates of employment and unemployment and on levels of participation in education and training gives only a partial picture of the nature of change. In the UK and elsewhere there are significant differences between the nature of the jobs that have been lost and many of those that have been created over the last two or three decades.

New forms of employment, especially in customer-facing roles and in the provision of personal services, usually need different skills and dispositions to those required by production industry. Moreover the nature of the employment relationship tends to differ significantly. Work in much of the service sector tends to be part-time, temporary or casualised. Pay and job security are often poor, and levels of trade union membership are generally lower. Downward pressure on terms and conditions, as well as intensified competition to secure employment more generally, have been increased by a number of broad trends in the labour market. Amongst these is a long-term increase in the number of women entering the workforce, especially those with children. There is also a growing proportion of older people continuing to work or returning to work whilst in semi-retirement. In addition, the first decade of the twenty-first century has seen a substantial increase in immigration into the UK, particularly from Central and Eastern Europe and Africa, but also from other parts of the world. From a Marxist perspective, the net result of these trends is that the reserve army of labour is increased and capital has a larger unit of labour to exploit.

The function of the reserve army of labour is twofold: firstly, employers are able to expand production without significant increases in labour costs; secondly, it disciplines the existing workforce. If labour is not sufficiently cheap or compliant, employers are able to use the threat of substitution. Such processes carry particular potency in post-industrial capitalism where low-skill service labour is generally expendable and relatively easy to replace (Byrne, 2005:42). Byrne (2005:106-107) describes a threefold division in patterns of work developing in the UK. At the bottom end of the labour market he identifies a pool of labour alternating between worklessness, low-waged, unrewarding and insecure employment, and various training and retraining courses. In the mid-1980s, Coffield *et al* (1986) described this scenario rather more bluntly: 'shit jobs and Govvy schemes' were seen as the most likely alternatives to unemployment for those at the bottom end of the labour market.

Above this group is a category of workers who are generally more qualified and employed on relatively favourable terms, although still poorly paid in comparison to less well-qualified workers in the previous generation. Finally, Byrne identifies a small group, of perhaps less than 10 per cent, enjoying an improved position. Although there are some new entrants into this group from below, most young people in this category inherit privilege. The elite have benefited most from the labour market changes that characterise post-industrial capitalism. Meanwhile, certain forms of education have effectively become a form of warehousing for young people attempting to obtain the credentials they believe will help them to avoid membership of a so-called under-class at the bottom of society (Ainley and Allen, 2010:76).

One effect of the changing nature of industry and employment in the UK is that it is no longer possible to identify or define a coherent youth labour market. What does exist, however, is an economy dominated by poor-quality work. Nevertheless, there are notable features relating to the employment of young workers. The relative earnings of young people have declined since the 1970s. In 1975, 16-year-olds typically earned 45 per cent of the UK national average wage, whilst the earnings of 25-year-olds equalled the national average. In contrast, by the end of the twentieth century, these figures had dropped to 38 per cent and 84 per cent of average earnings respectively. Much of this deterioration can be attributed to de-industrialisation, the associated demise of tradi-tional apprenticeships, the concomitant reductions in craft work, and the decline of other forms of skilled working-class employment (Bynner *et al*, 2002:5-6).

Conceptualising contemporary transitions

As a result of the far-reaching changes discussed above, it has been argued that attempting to understand the lives of young people through normative sequences is now inappropriate. Some sociologists argue that standardised, predictable youth transitions are associated with the social and economic conditions of a bygone age. The changes of the last thirty years have led some commentators to argue that we are now living in a new and different era; some describe this as a post-modern age, whilst others believe we are now in a state of late modernity (Jones, 2009:90). Either way, much research on the lives of young people has shifted away from structural understandings based largely on social class and the nature of the transitions from school to work that were once popular. Jeffs and Smith (1998) question the very currency of the term youth transitions, which they see as lacking mean-ing and value in contemporary society. They argue that traditional versions of the passage of young people into adulthood are out-dated as they are based largely on economic conceptions of the school to work transition.

We have been asked to use the concept of transition in an array of re-constituted forms ... What they each share is a desperation to hold fast to notions of an imagined mainstream in which the majority of young people neatly go forward in a unidirectional way towards some magic moment when adulthood is conferred. As such they are aligned to a predominantly economistic view which, particularly for young men, sees full-time employment as a pivotal signifier of adulthood. (Jeffs and Smith, 1998:53)

Alternative ways of interpreting the lives of young people have developed in the light of such significant social change. Postmodern approaches to youth studies focus largely on issues of style and identity. Such matters have long been of interest to those seeking to understand the lives of young people. During the 1970s and 1980s, academics associated with the University of Birmingham's *Centre for Contemporary Cultural Studies* (CCCS) were concerned with youth subcultures, but much of the CCCS work conceptualised the formation of culture and subculture within a structured framework of systematic social inequalities. In contrast, postmodern understandings tend to take a rather atomised, individualistic view of identity rather than seeing the life chances of particular groups as shaped by social structures and economic forces. For postmodernists, rapid social changes, particularly in the labour market and the industrial infrastructure of western societies, have led to a pervasive uncertainty. Consequently, social relations are no longer seen as linear or rational but based upon transitory meanings and accelerated change (Baudrillard, 1998).

Whereas it is argued that social life in modernist societies, such as the UK in the 1950s and 1960s, was based largely upon relations of production and the structured, relatively predictable lifestyles and opportunities which flowed from these, postmodern understandings emphasise the importance of consumption, choice and style. The old certainties of tradition and community are believed to have been superseded by alternative forms of status and identity. Fashion, sport and the media, alongside various forms of conspicuous consumption, are seen to be important signifiers of identity in an increasingly fragmented society. Culture is seen to be dominated by transition and change as the causal mechanisms of modernist society recede (Baudrillard, 1990). As social structures are no longer fixed, life becomes a game of risk, intuition, and individual agency that is free from the bonds of community and the circumstances of tradition. The search for rationality and linear progression is futile and ultimately alienating under radically changed circumstances (Jones, 2009:70).

Maffesoli (1996) argues that, whilst social class has lost its significance, other forms of identity have emerged which offer the potential to provide individual and collective meaning. Alternative collective associations, perhaps based upon youth sub-culture, fashion or other forms of common interest are seen as offering a certain *tribal* appeal. Whilst participation in such groups may be fluid, intermittent and sometimes short-lived, Maffesoli believes they offer a collective experience which provides individuals with values and social support. It is questionable, however, whether such affiliations provide the basis for young people to build meaningful identities in a way that is comparable to peer group processes in the past (Jones, 2009:69). Bauman (1995) argues that groups such as Maffesoli's tribes cannot offer meaningful forms of collective identity because of the inherent uncertainties and anxieties that characterise the postmodern age.

Postmodern perspectives are not without value. Arguably, the traditional structural emphasis of much work on youth transitions tended to see young people as pawns, swept along by social and economic restructuring; and there is evidence that many young people do not readily identify with a particular social class. Often they do not expect their transitions to be linear or sequential (Cohen and Ainley, 2000:83); and the active ways in which young people negotiate their circumstances have generally been overlooked (Miles, 2000:10). We live in a consumerist society where fashion and style are sometimes fetishised. Changes in technology and the media mean that young people now exist in a complex social matrix where reality can sometimes blur with virtual experiences. For many young people, the notion that contemporary society is free from the old-fashioned divisions of social class holds an inherent appeal. The emancipatory promise of postmodernism, where the individual is free to create and recreate their own identity, is seductive.

As discussed in Chapter 1, young people often do not recognise the salience of social class or the importance of structural inequalities. However, this does not necessarily mean they do not exist or that they have ceased to be important. One could argue that the life chances of young people are affected more than ever by structural inequality. The concentration on identity entailed by postmodernism may deflect attention from the pernicious effects on young people of neo-liberalism. Whilst the world is undoubtedly more complex and difficult to understand than it was fifty years ago, society is not an amorphous jumble; social life does not take place within a socio-economic vacuum. There are a number of dangers which are inherent in a postmodern analysis: ultimately, the individual can become seen as lost in a malaise of superficial signs and symbols which are devoid of logic or meaning (Elliott, 2001: 140).

The work of Giddens (1991) and Beck (1992) offers a useful framework through which to consider the lives of young people in post-industrial capitalist societies. These authors acknowledge that western societies have undergone great change over recent decades, and recognise that the collective cultural experiences of the post-war era have largely been replaced by greater levels of individualisation. However, they argue that individualisation is not necessarily positive or empowering. Whilst many believe that lifestyle choices allow individuals to exercise agency, Giddens (1991:5) argues that individuals are compelled to make lifestyle choices, and Beck (1992) refers to enforced emancipation. Bourdieu (1984:379) sees working-class culture and consumption as bounded by 'the culture of the necessary'. These and similar analyses see individualisation as a product of capitalism in late modernity rather than being symptomatic of a new era of postmodernity. Indeed, Beck (1992:35) argues that, rather than leading to its collapse, the uncertainties and risks associated with individualisation have increased and polarised social class divisions.

The UK is now a less equal society than at any time since the end of the First World War; even official sources recognise that social mobility is severely limited (see, for example, the 2009 Cabinet Office report, *Unleashing Aspirations*). This is not only a problem for the socially excluded. Although most young people from middle-class backgrounds invest considerable amounts of time, effort and money in pursuing education and training, sometimes well into their twenties and beyond, the rewards traditionally associated with middle-class status have been appropriated by a small subset, leaving others at greater disadvantage

(Brown *et al*, 2011). Reflecting increasing public concern about the domination of high-status employment by young people from highly privileged backgrounds, the BBC documentary *Who Gets the Best Jobs?* (BBC, 2011) explained labour market inequalities in terms of varying levels of economic, social and cultural capital possessed by young people from different social class backgrounds. The opportunity bargain – where young people have been promised a future of prosperity and security in exchange for hard work and deferred gratification – is increasingly becoming an opportunity gap. As more and more highly qualified workers compete for a diminishing pool of high quality jobs, the elite enjoying extensive networks of advantage seize the best opportunities (Brown *et al*, 2011).

Young people, class and social exclusion

Social research, and perhaps youth studies especially, tends to over-emphasise social change. As Shildrick and MacDonald (2007:592) argue, continuity rarely attracts the same attention. Despite this, a significant amount of research draws attention to continuities in the way many young people view their journey into adulthood (MacDonald and Marsh, 2005; Nayak, 2006; Roberts, 2009a; Shildrick and MacDonald, 2007). Attitudes towards work and education in some of the UK's poorest neighbourhoods are remarkably durable. Despite changes in the labour market and the education system, there is still evidence of the widespread negativity towards school that Willis (1977) found in young working-class people over thirty years ago. The forms of work or training sought by school leavers also tend to be quite traditional, and to reflect long-established patterns of class and gender difference. Choice and ambition are still heavily influenced and constrained by family and peer group norms and expectations (MacDonald *et al*, 2005). Often, young men still aspire to jobs as motor mechanics, construction workers or soldiers, whilst many young women choose hairdressing, child care and secretarial work. Whilst many young people in deprived areas participate in post-compulsory education and training, either voluntarily or through compulsion, retention and completion rates are often low (Shildrick and MacDonald, 2007).

Although engagement in some form of post-compulsory education and training is now the norm for most young people, in the main participation continues to reflect ingrained patterns of class and gender differentiation. Nayak's ethnographic studies (2003; 2006), carried out in the north-east of England, have found that social class is of continuing salience, especially for young working-class men. Although Nayak recognises that traditional patterns of work, especially for males, have changed greatly, he also highlights a remarkable durability in working-class attitudes, values and dispositions. Whilst nowadays the sons of fitters, sheet-metal workers and engineers are more likely to be employed in shops, offices and various other parts of the service sector, Nayak (2006:815) sees these young men as transposing older working-class values onto new conditions in new times

> [W]hile social class may rarely be discussed directly by young people it continues to be threaded through the daily fabric of their lives: it is stitched into codes of respect, accent, dress, music, bodily adornment and comportment. In short, the affective politics of class is a felt practice, tacitly understood and deeply internalised ... Despite major economic transformation and media re-branding, the cultures of the old industrial city and the identities therein refuse to be written out of existence (Nayak, 2006:828).

Changes in the economy and the labour market have led to increasing social polarisation – not only *between* the working-class and other social classes but also *within* the different social classes. This manifests itself in many ways but, as far as the working-classes are concerned, it is possible to discern a growing divide between what might traditionally have been described as the rough and respectable working-classes. Such divisions are not new and can be traced back to Victorian notions of the deserving and the undeserving poor. Whilst socially excluded young people may nowadays be ridiculed as chavs or charvers, or assigned other derogatory labels, there have always been demarcations and cultural fragments within social class groupings (Nayak, 2006). Chav and other such terms are associated with the reproduction and re-constitution of the working-class in a post-industrial society, and can be understood as cultural expressions of historic social divisions in a post-industrial context.

Attachment to place and social networks based on a particular locality are important influences on young people's life choices (MacDonald *et al*, 2005; Green and White, 2008). Class and family backgrounds provide young people with particular forms of social and cultural capital, rooted in local economic circumstances and regional identities (Forrest and Kearns, 2001); consequently, individual choices about educational and economic participation are 'based on subjective values and aspirations, which, in turn, may be constrained by objective opportunities available to individuals at local level' (Green and White, 2008:213). This geographical structuring of perceptions and employment conditions, often at a very fine spatial scale, produces geographies of opportunity – both subjective and objective – which have particular significance for participation.

Despite all the changes of the last thirty years, the ambitions of most young people are still quite traditional. Many of today's teenagers, just like those of preceding generations, want to be in employment, to earn decent wages and to be treated as adults (Wolf, 2011:20). Roberts (2009a:118) argues that youth transition is still a useful concept which can help us to understand the lives of young people. After all, most of them do still eventually gain full-time employment; the majority aspire to conventional adult lifestyles and will form nuclear families.

For those from privileged backgrounds there are clear continuities of advantage and, in some ways, these advantages have increased and intensified. In England, levels of educational participation and attainment have always been significantly greater for the higher social classes, who tend to access high status forms of learning and the most prestigious institutions (Ball, 2003). Furthermore, although educational attainment has risen across all social groups, there continues to be significant variation and inequality in the level and type of qualifications gained by individuals from different backgrounds. Patterns of inequality are perhaps most visible in the state-private school divide, but they are also present in post-compulsory education. Although it is now the norm for most young people to continue their education beyond the minimum school leaving age of 16, there are marked differences in the nature of this experience, based upon forms of difference such as gender and ethnicity, and particularly social class.

Those from privileged backgrounds have considerable advantages over their contemporaries, and are able to capitalise on and mobilise these advantages in various ways. Whereas previously the transitions of middle and upper-middle class young people into well-paid and secure careers were fairly predictable, significantly increased participation in higher education has intensified competition and led to higher levels of anxiety and uncertainty. Increasingly, parental influence extends from school into university and course choices, but also into various other parts of their children's lives, whether this is help in securing an internship, assisting with property purchase, or using their influence and connections to help their children to secure permanent employment. Whatever forms such parenting takes, it constitutes another form of class advantage (Ainley and Allen, 2010:116-117).

Since the 1980s, the policies of successive governments have exacerbated rather than ameliorated the differing experience of participation for individuals from different social classes. Virtually all forms of education and training have been subject to commercialisation and marketisation and, as Ball (2003) argues, in an educational marketplace those with the highest levels of economic, cultural and social capital are best able to manipulate systems of educational selection and allocation which claim to be neutral. In the complicated jungle of educational qualifications and institutions that characterises the English education system, notions of diversity and choice become highly stratified according to social class and other forms of difference, not least in the distinction between vocational and academic learning.

The Wolf *Review of Vocational Education* (2011) confirms what most experts know and many of the public have long suspected – that low-level vocational qualifications have little labour market value. Whilst, for most, general academic education is still the favoured option, some apprenticeships, particularly higher level provision run by large employers, offer viable alternatives for young people able to secure a place. However, Wolf argues that many young people get little economic benefit from the education system, highlighting the 350,000 16 to 19-year-olds on low-level vocational programmes which fail to promote progression into stable, paid employment or enable access to higher level education and training in a consistent or effective way (Wolf, 2011:21). Thus, whilst elite forms of education offer clear social and economic advantages, participation in low-status forms of education and training may contribute to exclusion and disadvantage.

61

4

Young People not in Education, Employment or Training

This chapter reviews existing knowledge regarding young people not in education, employment or training. Although NEET as a construct of UK education policy is a response to specific social and political circumstances, it is paralleled by similar concerns elsewhere, and the discussion draws on international literature as well as work in the UK. Our focus is primarly on England, and the experience of other countries is used mainly to support and amplify the points being made. The chapter begins by tracing the development of NEET as an analytical category and mapping the structure of the NEET population. We then consider the evidence on how young people come to be in this category, taking a critical view of some of the factors used to explain non-participation and highlighting the socially constructed nature of notions such as achievement and disaffection. The advantages and disadvantages of discourses based on the NEET category are examined. So are the consequences in later life of being outside education and the labour market as a young person. We conclude by reviewing two key policy initiatives aimed at increasing participation rates: Connexions and the Educational Maintenance Allowance (EMA).

Too young and too precious to waste

The emergence of NEET as a way of thinking about young people can be traced back to the changes in youth labour markets discussed in Chapter 3, and the consequent increases in educational participation rates. As policy responses became increasingly focused on establishing post-compulsory education or training as the norm, 16 and 17-year-olds were no longer seen as independent agents, entitled to seek work and to claim benefits in their own right. In a period of public expenditure reductions, direct state support for young people was progressively reduced. When YTS was introduced in 1983, it contained benefit sanctions for those refusing to take up a place, and for young people in education financial support such as Supplementary Benefit became increasingly difficult to obtain. In 1988, National Insurance regulations changed so that unemployment benefit was available only after two years of contributions, effectively excluding those under 18. In the same year, the Social Security Act removed entitlement to means-tested benefits from most 16-17 year olds and made YTS compulsory for unemployed young people in this age group. YTS - Youth Training Scheme

Although participation rates continued to grow into the 1990s, those who remained outside education, training and employment disappeared from official statistics. This led researchers and government officials to look for new ways of monitoring the extent of labour market vulnerability amongst young people (Furlong, 2006). The expression 'not in education, training or employment' – the positions of training and employment are reversed in our current terminology – was used in the pioneering study of NEET young people in South Glamorgan (Istance *et al*, 1994). This research also referred to participants as 'Status 0', a classification derived from careers service records but carrying more emotive overtones. Williamson (2010) describes how, in 1996, a senior Home Office official coined the acronym NEET in preference to Status 0, which had met with some hostility in government circles, perhaps because of its use as 'a metaphor for young people who, in policy terms, at the time counted for nothing and were going nowhere' (*ibid*).

The South Glamorgan study estimated that between 16 per cent and 23 per cent of 16 to 17-year-olds were in Status 0 and argued that both supply and demand factors were implicated in these high figures, identifying problematic individual transitions to adulthood and structural conditions in the job market as significant issues. The Government was wrong-footed by public interest in the issue, and was unable to supply data to refute or confirm these statistics (Hansard, 1994). However, the political neglect of these young people was not to last much longer, and the focus on social exclusion developed by New Labour in the years preceding the 1997 general election prepared the way for a period of unprecedented attention to this group. As Tony Blair stated in his foreword to *Bridging the Gap*, the report on NEET young people commissioned by the incoming government:

> The best defence against social exclusion is having a job, and the best way to get a job is to have a good education, with the right training and experience ... But every year some 161,000 young people between 16 and 18 are not involved in any education, training or employment. For the majority these are wasted and frustrating years that lead, inexorably, to lower pay and worse job prospects in later life ... Getting this right offers the prospect of a double dividend. A better life for young people themselves, saving them from the prospect of a lifetime of dead-end jobs, unemployment, poverty, ill-health and other kinds of exclusion. A better deal for society as a whole that has to pay a very high price in terms of welfare bills and crime for failing to help people make the transition to becoming independent adults.' (SEU, 1999:6)

The assumptions of this discourse have already been questioned in Chapter 2, and are examined in detail later in this chapter. However, it is worth noting at this point the characteristic dual narrative of NEET policy, in which unoccupied young people are simultaneously regarded as *in trouble*, requiring intervention to prevent negative consequences now and in later life, but also *as trouble*. According to a newspaper article at the time of the South Glamorgan study (McRae, 1994) these 16 to 18-year-olds are 'Too young and too precious to waste'. At the same time, however, they are seen as constituting a threat to society, either as a drain on resources or more directly through engagement in criminal or antisocial activity. Another early study, conducted in the north-east of England, noted fears 'that these young people are out of control and ... have turned parts of our cities and housing estates into no-go areas' (Wilkinson, 1995:1). At a time of extensive political and media interest in the emergence of a so-called underclass, the idea that cultures of worklessness and welfare dependency would take root in a new generation of young people made NEET an issue that was impossible to ignore.

Estimating the numbers of NEET young people

Providing reliable estimates of the size and composition of the NEET population is not straightforward. Being NEET is often a dynamic experience in which periods of inactivity are interspersed with engagement in training programmes, college courses or casual employment. The turnover between various forms of participation and non-participation is referred to as *churning*, and although the proportion of young people who are NEET for long periods is significant, many young people change status in any given month. This volatile situation complicates the collection and interpretation of data, and snapshot figures taken at different times of the year vary considerably, with particular peaks and troughs at the beginning and end of the academic year. Furlong (2006) and Bynner and Parsons (2002) discuss some of these difficulties, and the consequences of different definitions for understanding the NEET population.

In England, official figures for NEET young people are currently estimated by first calculating the number outside education and training from the known 16-18 population and the number of enrolled learners. The Labour Force Survey (LFS) is then used to estimate what proportion of this group is not in employment. Both annual and quarterly estimates are produced. According to these official figures, NEET rates for 16 to 18-year-olds have been remarkably constant over many years, remaining at around 9-10 per cent since 1994. Table 4.1 contains end-of-year estimates between 1998 and 2008, together with the rates for different forms of participation, such as employment, full-time education and work-based learning. Table 4.2 provides more detailed information for the end of 2008, by age and gender. In both tables, age is identified according to the academic year convention which classifies young people by their age on the previous 31st August. Official statistics on 16 to 18-year-olds may therefore include some young people whose chronological age is 19.

There is considerable geographical variation in NEET rates, which tend to be higher in areas of deprivation and high unemployment. However, there are many exceptions, often due to missing data but also because specific local circumstances, such as the availability of seasonal and casual work, can result in unexpectedly high or low figures. Table 4.3 shows NEET rates by region in England, together with the highest local

66

percentage

End of calendar year	1998	1999	2000	2001	2002	2003	2004	2005	2006	2007	2008
Category of Education or Training											
Full-time education	55.8	56.9	57.0	56.1	56.6	56.7	57.9	59.7	61.4	62.5	64.7
Work Based Learning (WBL)	9.6	9.4	9.3	8.5	8.0	8.1	7.7	7.3	6.7	6.8	6.6
Employer Funded Training (EFT)	5.7	5.6	4.8	5.0	5.0	5.1	4.8	4.6	4.5	4.5	3.9
Other Education and Training (OET)	5.3	5.1	5.6	5.7	5.7	5.6	5.4	5.1	4.7	4.5	4.6
Total Education and Training	**76.0**	**76.7**	**76.5**	**75.1**	**75.0**	**75.3**	**75.7**	**76.5**	**77.1**	**78.0**	**79.7**
Not in any education or training – in employment	14.7	15.1	14.8	15.0	15.0	15.2	14.7	12.8	12.5	12.3	10.1
Not in any education, employment or training (NEET)	**9.2**	**8.1**	**8.7**	**9.9**	**10.0**	**9.5**	**9.6**	**10.7**	**10.4**	**9.7**	**10.3**
Total Not in any Education or Training (NET)	24.0	23.3	23.5	24.9	25.0	24.7	24.3	23.5	22.9	22.0	20.3
Population (thousands)	1,804	1,786	1,790	1,847	1,892	1,935	1,969	1,994	2,013	2,017	2,018

Table 4.1: Participation of 16-18 year olds in education and training in England 1998-2008
Adapted from Statistical First Release SFR 18/2010 (DfE, 2010a)

percentage

	Age 16		Age 17		Age 18		Age 16-18		All
	M	F	M	F	M	F	M	F	
Category of Education or Training									
Full-time education	79.2	86.2	64.4	73.2	40.2	47.3	61.0	68.7	64.7
Work Based Learning (WBL)	6.7	4.4	8.8	6.0	8.6	4.9	8.0	5.1	6.6
Employer Funded Training (EFT)	1.9	1.4	4.0	2.7	7.7	5.2	4.6	3.1	3.9
Other Education and Training (OET)	4.3	3.2	5.0	4.3	5.6	5.3	5.0	4.3	4.6
Total Education and Training	**91.8**	**95.0**	**81.9**	**86.1**	**61.9**	**62.6**	**78.3**	**81.1**	**79.7**
Not in any education or training – in employment	2.4	1.5	8.9	5.4	20.0	21.5	10.5	9.6	10.1
Not in any education, employment or training (NEET)	**5.8**	**3.5**	**9.2**	**8.5**	**18.1**	**15.8**	**11.1**	**9.3**	**10.3**
Total Not in any Education or Training (NET)	8.2	5.0	18.1	13.9	38.1	37.4	21.7	18.9	20.3
Population (thousands)	338.9	318.5	349.2	326.8	353.2	330.9	1,041.5	976.3	2,017.5

Table 4.2: Participation of 16-18 year olds in education and training in England at end of calendar year 2008
Adapted from Statistical First Release SFR 18/2010 (DfE, 2010a)

16-18 year olds known to be NEET

	Estimated number	% of all 16-18 year olds known to Connexions	Highest rate in region (%)	% of 16-18 year olds whose current activity is not known
South East	14,690	5.7	9.9	5.9
London	12,090	5.8	10.0	5.0
East of England	11,360	6.2	9.1	4.2
South West	9,180	5.7	8.2	3.0
West Midlands	13,000	7.0	11.9	4.3
East Midlands	8,040	5.4	8.4	4.1
Yorkshire and Humber	14,080	7.9	10.6	6.7
North West	19,440	7.8	10.5	3.3
North East	9,010	9.8	13.2	4.4

Table 4.3: NEET rates in England by region, 2008

Source: http://www.dcsf.gov.uk/14-19/documents/NEET2008.xls (Excel spreadsheet)

authority rates for each region. The percentage of young people whose status is not known is included, although this figure varies substantially and in some local authorities can be as many as one in five.

The difficulties of monitoring overall numbers of NEET young people are compounded when more detailed information is required, such as the length of time spent NEET or the nature of previous activities. Although in theory Connexions is responsible for maintaining contact with young people and recording data on their activities, the complexity of post-compulsory provision and the possibility that contact may be lost mean that, in practice, information is somewhat incomplete. Important UK sources for this more detailed knowledge include large-scale surveys such as the Youth Cohort Study (YCS), the Longitudinal Study of Young People in England (LSYPE), and the Scottish School Leavers Survey (SSLS). Connexions maintains an activity database and reports regularly to central government. In addition, the British Household Panel Survey and the LFS provide useful information.

Structure of the NEET population

The NEET category is defined negatively, comprising those who are outside education or the labour market for reasons that may be highly complex and diverse. When used in the context of 16 to 18-year-olds, it combines age groups in a significant way, as policy and interventions in England often distinguish between 16 to 17-year-olds and those who are 18 or over. The increasing use of NEET to refer to unemployed 18 to 24-year-olds compounds this. Consequently, the NEET population is highly diverse, both in terms of the challenges young people face and the length of time they spend outside education and employment. Although it is important to understand that this diversity is partly a policy construct, a result of grouping together a variety of different experiences and conditions under a single heading, research into the structure of the NEET population can be valuable.

Factors involved in non-participation and the circumstances affecting young people have been mapped in detail by a substantial literature on NEET sub-groups, in which young people are classified according to characteristics seen as particularly relevant in terms of framing policy or planning interventions (Scottish Executive, 2006; NFER, 2009). However, Finlay et al (2010) argue that the sub-group concept is unhelpful, warn-

in percentages		16-17	18-24
Looking for work or suitable course	44	38	
Waiting to start a job/course	14	6	
Pregnant or caring for own children	8	27	
Disability or ill health	7	11	
Gap year before higher education	5	2	
Caring for a dependant adult relative	<1	1	
Refugee or asylum seeker	1	<1	
Doing unpaid/voluntary work	<1	1	
Other reason	20	13	

Table 4.4: Main reason for being NEET at ages 16-17 and 18-24
Adapted from DCSF (2009:12)

ing that the presence in the NEET category of young people with particular characteristics does not imply the existence of relatively homogeneous sub-groups with similar needs and responses. For example, teenage parents share one specific characteristic but may have widely differing responses to their situation and have various different requirements for support. Interventions need to be planned at an individual level that take into account the combination of circumstances and attributes of each person.

Young people may be NEET for subjective reasons or because of more or less objective circumstances, although there is not always a clear distinction between the two. For example, they may regard further education as unhelpful and regard any work available to them as too low-paid to be worthwhile. In other cases, participation in work or study may be prevented by ill-health or caring responsibilities. Combinations of subjective and objective circumstances are common. Table 4.4, based on LFS data from 2009, indicates some of the main explanations given by young people for non-participation, and the size of each sub-group in England at ages 16 or 17 and 18 to 24.

percentages	Full-time education	Job with training	Job without training	Government-supported training	NEET	Weighted base
White	61	10	13	8	8	14,185
Mixed	67	7	13	4	8	376
Indian	90	2	3	1	3	382
Pakistani	79	5	4	3	9	392
Bangladeshi	79	2	6	4	9	164
Other Asian	89	*	*	*	4	200
Black African	91	3	2	1	3	304
Black Caribbean	75	4	7	3	1	241
Other	84	5	4	1	6	173

Table 4.5: Main activity at age 17 by ethnicity
Adapted from DCSF/ONS (2009:30)

As might be expected, the largest single group in both age groups comprises those who are seeking work or a suitable course of further education. The size of this group is sensitive to local labour market conditions and the availability of educational opportunities; traditional patterns of delivery in schools and colleges can extend waiting times for young people who wish to return to study. Figure 4.1 (see page 74) provides similar data for 17-year-olds in Scotland, based on the Scottish School Leavers Survey (Furlong, 2006). These data provide a somewhat more refined analysis of the reasons for non-participation and allow for more than one reason to be given; again, seeking suitable work or education were the most commonly cited reasons for being NEET, and nearly 40 per cent of respondents identified a need for more qualifications or skills. In both England and Scotland, ill health, disability and personal or family problems were cited by a much smaller but still significant proportion as major constraints.

Overall, NEET rates are gendered and increase with age. Data for England in 2008 show that 3.5 per cent of young women and 5.8 per cent of young men were NEET at age 16; however, for 17-year-olds non-participation was significantly greater and the gender gap smaller as a proportion of overall rates, the corresponding figures being 8.5 per cent and 9.2 per cent (see Table 4.2). By the age of 18, when many young people have completed courses or apprenticeships, NEET rates in Table 4.2 show a further increase: almost doubling from the figures at age 17. For 16 to 24-year-olds as a whole, rates are higher for women than for men (Social Exclusion Task Force, 2009). Differences between male and female respondents are most evident where participation is made difficult by pregnancy or looking after their own children. Unsurprisingly, this is the most important single reason reported by young women for being NEET, at age 17 outweighing both lack of qualifications and insufficient experience (DCSF/ONS, 2009). In Scotland, homemaking or childcare were reported as major obstacles to participation by nearly 20 per cent of NEET young women aged 17, but only around 3 per cent in the case of young men. As young people grow older, the increasing importance of children as a factor in non-participation is clear – see Table 4.4 (page 71).

Variations in NEET rates between ethnic groups are complex and show similar variations to the ethnic differences in educational attainment

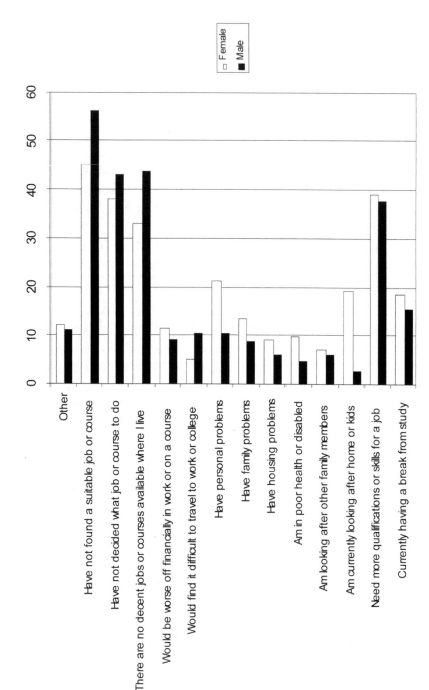

Figure 4.1: Reasons for currently being NEET at age 17 in Scotland, 2003 (by percentage)
Source: Furlong (2006:561).

outlined in Chapter 1. Those of Black African or Indian descent are considerably less likely than other ethnic groups to be NEET at age 17, whilst Pakistani, Bangladeshi and Black Caribbean groups have slightly higher rates than those from white or mixed backgrounds (DCSF/ONS, 2009). In Table 4.5, the main activity of young people aged 17 is broken down by ethnic group, revealing the interaction of factors such as propensity to engage in full-time education and the likelihood of obtaining different forms of employment. For example, although young people from Black Caribbean backgrounds are considerably more likely to be engaged in full-time education than those of white descent, employment rates and engagement in government-supported training are much lower for the former group. This illustrates the principle that NEET rates for specific ages are not necessarily strongly coupled to employment prospects; certain groups of young people may react to adverse labour market conditions by remaining in education for longer, although this may simply defer unemployment.

The specific circumstances of NEET young people are closely related to their prospects of resuming participation in the fairly near future. Analysis of YCS data identifies three broad groups in this respect (NFER, 2009). Around 41 per cent of NEET young people were 'open to learning' and likely to return to education or training in the short term; these people tended to have higher levels of educational attainment and more positive attitudes to learning. A further 38 per cent were 'sustained NEET' and unlikely to re-engage, even in the medium term; they tended to have lower attainment and negative experiences of school, and higher levels of truancy and exclusion during their school careers. The remainder were identified as 'undecided NEET'; they shared many of the features of the 'open to learning' group and disengagement seemed largely a result of dissatisfaction with the opportunities available to them rather than with disaffection. Thus, for around three-quarters of NEET young people aged 16 to 18, re-engagement is likely to occur either with minimal intervention or by providing more attractive opportunities. For the remainder, significant levels of support and long-term interventions aimed at restoring – or perhaps more accurately, creating – confidence and enjoyment in learning is likely to be an expensive pre-requisite for re-engagement.

Being and becoming: underlying risks of becoming NEET

For many young people, exclusion from education and labour markets is both an outcome and a continuing part of social and educational disadvantage, leading to further negative consequences in later life. Family poverty and deprivation profoundly affect young people's prospects, increasing the likelihood of disaffection and educational underachievement. More generally, the interaction of class, gender and race within a changing matrix of economic and social circumstances produces a range of categories which structure the chances of joining the NEET group. This section examines the factors involved and the ways in which they are related to structures of inequality within society.

From the outset of research into this issue, a recurrent theme has been that high-risk groups are likely to be characterised by disadvantaged family backgrounds and poor school experiences, often exacerbated by the depressed condition of local labour markets and the stigma attaching to deprived neighbourhoods. In the South Glamorgan study, many young people had low self-esteem as a result of unsuccessful school careers, which had often led to sustained truancy. They frequently had little expectation of getting what some referred to as a proper job, as opposed to a place on a training scheme.

In a parallel study of non-participation in disadvantaged estates in Sunderland (Wilkinson, 1995), many of the themes highlighted in Wales emerged again. Wilkinson stressed the importance of the lack of job opportunities for young people, suggesting that job creation on a significant scale was needed to alleviate social exclusion. The shortage of decent jobs was a recurring theme, and was often a significant factor in low self-esteem and restricted aspirations. In terms of individual experience, the same complex picture of multiple disadvantage emerged, and poverty, problems at school, perceived lack of careers advice and negative perceptions of training schemes all contributed to exclusion at an early age.

Research in Northern Ireland at around the same time showed similar patterns to those in the North-East and in Wales, but found a somewhat lower incidence of non-participation than in these areas (Armstrong *et al*, 1997). Other early studies included *Wasted Youth* (Pearce and Hillman, 1998), as well as quantitative analysis of data from the YCS (Payne 1999) and the British Cohort Study of 1970 (Bynner and Parsons, 2002).

Summarising this growing body of research, *Bridging the Gap* identified three overlapping groups of young people with a significantly higher risk of becoming NEET: those whose parents are poor or unemployed; members of some (but not all) ethnic minority groups; and young people in circumstances likely to create barriers to participation. The latter group includes young people with a learning difficulty, disability or long-term illness, those in or leaving care, young offenders and those involved in drug or alcohol misuse, as well as teenage parents, carers and homeless young people.

More recent studies identify the same groups of young people as continuing to bear the greatest risk of social exclusion. Indeed, one of the striking features of research into NEET young people is how little has changed since the early 1990s. Although unemployment, family breakdown, and involvement with drug-taking and criminal activity affect young people from all sectors of society, those in disadvantaged or deprived circumstances are least able to access the material and cultural resources to mitigate their effects. These problems are intensified by educational underachievement, itself strongly associated with social disadvantage, and policy interventions based on neo-liberal assumptions have had limited success in compensating for the cumulative effects of disadvantage and changes in employment structures. Consequently, there is remarkable continuity in the findings of successive studies into the risk factors associated with becoming NEET.

Educational achievement and educational disadvantage

Although the relationship between achievement and participation is complex and mediated by gender and ethnicity, qualification levels are a major factor in post-16 educational choices (Payne, 2003), and also affect the chances of obtaining employment. In England, being NEET at age 17 is four times more common amongst those with no qualifications than for those who achieve the relatively modest level of one to four grades A*-C at GCSE, and nearly twenty times the rate of those with eight or more grades A*-C (DCSF/ONS, 2009). Researchers in other countries also report an association with low educational attainment, for example in Australia (Hillman, 2005), Japan (Genda, 2007) and Scotland (Furlong, 2006).

Using longitudinal data on a cohort of people born in Great Britain in 1970, Bynner and Parsons (2002) found that young people with no qualifications were six times more likely to be NEET than those with 'O' level qualifications or above. However, this relationship was gendered: girls with no qualifications were less likely to become NEET than boys. Ethnicity also modifies the relationship between achievement and participation, and there is evidence that young people from certain ethnic minority groups are more likely than their white peers to participate in full-time post-compulsory education, in spite of lower average levels of educational attainment amongst young people from Pakistani, Bangladeshi and Black Caribbean backgrounds (DCSF/ONS, 2009).

It is important to recognise that achievement differentials according to class, race and gender are partly a social construction, in which dominant notions of educational success privilege certain forms of achievement at the expense of others, which in consequence are marginalised and devalued. Policy discussion on achievement tends to focus on measurable outcomes such as the number and level of qualifications obtained and improving examination performance. The more holistic models of achievement are neglected and discourses of educational success are constructed which exclude and problematise certain groups of people, particularly white working-class boys and Black Caribbeans.

Archer (2008:89) argues that policy discourse in this area is 'overwhelmingly concerned with the notion of *under*achievement', concentrating largely on mapping risk factors and potential cures rather than analysing conditions for success. However, we must also acknowledge that, whilst constructions of success and variations in terms of gender and ethnicity are important, young people who underachieve in educational terms will generally be at greater risk of becoming NEET. Educational disadvantage – systematic inequality in the processes or outcomes of education – is undoubtedly an important contributor to NEET rates.

Disadvantage may arise as a consequence of individual attributes, such as having a learning difficulty or disability, or from family circumstances: for example, being in care. However, such circumstances are not unrelated to wider social structures, and young people from poorer families are disproportionately likely to have special educational needs or to have been in care (Cassen and Kingdon, 2007). The invisibility of

Parents' occupation	Weighted base	Level 2 at 16 (%)	Level 2 at 17 (%)	% without Level 2 at age 16 gaining it by 17	% without Level 2 at 17
Higher professional	1,129	81	88	33	12
Lower professional	6,193	75	82	28	18
Intermediate	3,097	61	71	26	29
Lower supervisory	1,353	47	58	20	42
Routine	2,787	43	54	20	46
Other/not classified	1,957	37	49	19	51

Table 4.6: Level 2 attainment at 16 and 17 by social class
Adapted from DCSF/ONS (2009:30)

Parents' occupation	Full-time education	Job with training	Job without training	Government-supported training	NEET	NEET as proportion of those outside FT education
Higher professional	78	6	7	5	3	14
Lower professional	73	8	9	6	3	12
Intermediate	61	10	14	9	6	15
Lower supervisory	50	13	17	12	9	18
Routine	50	10	17	9	14	28
Other/not classified	57	7	11	7	18	42

Table 4.7: Main activity at 17 by parental occupation (percentage)
Adapted from DCSF/ONS (2009:30)

certain ethnic minorities through absorption into a white working-class category – for example, the Gypsy/Roma group, whose underachievement is particularly notable – can also lead to some forms of ethnic disadvantage being overlooked. Recent discourses on underachieving boys reflect changing patterns of gender disadvantage in education (Francis, 2006) although, as we pointed out in Chapter 1, they largely differentiate within social classes rather than between them (Francis and Skelton, 2005). Similarly, framing the white working-class as a disadvantaged *ethnic* group has tended to divert attention not only from the continuing disadvantage of some ethnic minorities, but also from the underlying class basis of educational attainment.

Social class remains the strongest predictor of educational achievement in the UK, a society where class differences in achievement are amongst the highest in the Western world (Perry and Francis, 2010). In England, YCS and LSYPE data show that attainment at age 16 and 17 is highly structured by class, with clear gradients in the percentages achieving Level 2 both in school and in post-compulsory education (see Table 4.6). Unsurprisingly, there is also a strong association between socio-economic status (SES) and becoming NEET (DCSF/ONS, 2009). Young people from low-SES backgrounds are significantly more likely to be NEET and to spend substantial periods in this category than those from professional backgrounds (see Tables 4.7 and 4.8). When other indicators of family social position are used, a similar picture emerges. Children receiving free school meals in their final year of compulsory schooling are considerably more likely to become NEET after leaving school than others (DCSF/ONS, 2009). Conversely, Coles *et al* (2002) note that the young people least likely to be NEET are those living with two parents in owner-occupied housing with a father working full time. However, although its influence on the chances of becoming NEET is strong, class appears to operate indirectly in shaping early labour market outcomes, operating largely through levels of educational achievement in countries across Europe (Ianelli and Smyth, 2008).

Using a statistical analysis of data from BCS70, Bynner and Parsons (2002) found little independent effect from social class, but significant contributions from a small number of related factors which also showed intriguing differences between the sexes, including specific aspects of material disadvantage. After educational achievement, which showed

Parent's occupation	None	1-3 months	4-12 months	12+ months	Average time NEET for those who have been NEET
(months)					
Higher professional	93	3	4	<1	<1
Lower professional	90	3	5	1	7
Intermediate	85	5	8	3	8
Lower supervisory	78	6	11	5	9
Routine	72	7	14	7	9
Other/not classified	69	5	16	11	11

Table 4.8: Percentage of months NEET by parents' occupation
Adapted from DCSF/ONS (2009)

the strongest effect for both males and females, living on a council estate or inner-city housing was most important for young men, whilst for women family poverty, indicated by eligibility for free school meals or particular state benefits, had the greatest influence. This suggests that family circumstances and experience add to educational achievement, rather than simply operating through it, in influencing post-16 participation (Bynner and Parsons, 2002). That is, for young people from working-class backgrounds with similar levels of educational achievement, the likelihood of becoming NEET is further increased by factors such as poor housing and poverty.

The low NEET rates amongst young people from high-SES backgrounds are largely a consequence of greater participation in full-time education. Leaving education to seek work increases the likelihood of becoming NEET even for those who are relatively privileged (Thompson, 2011a). When non-participation rates are calculated as a proportion of young people not in full-time education (see the final column of Table 4.7), social class differences are less marked and labour market prospects are grim for young people from all backgrounds. Similarly, only NEET young people from higher professional backgrounds spend considerably less time, on average, in this category than others, again suggesting that the risks of seeking employment at an early age are not confined to low-SES groups (Table 4.8). Nevertheless, these risks are unequally distributed, and even amongst those who enter the labour market early, NEET rates are substantially higher for young people from low-SES backgrounds than for their more privileged peers. Furthermore, although social class differences in the average length of time outside education or the labour market are generally not large, the likelihood of spending more than twelve months NEET is much greater for low-SES young people than for those from professional backgrounds.

In England, having the qualifications required to progress to academic study, and ultimately to higher education, appears to be a key factor in participation. In 2008, almost 80 per cent of NEET young people had qualifications below the level normally expected for such progression (five or more GCSE passes at grades A*-C). However, the fact that lower achievers are much more likely to become NEET does not imply that most NEET young people will have very low levels of qualification. In England the effects of educational expansion and credential inflation mean that leaving school with no GCSE passes, or very low grades, is comparatively rare. Conversely, many more school leavers now attain a high level of qualification; although the proportion of these young people who become NEET is small, the group as a whole is large enough that those who leave school and do not find work is numerically significant. As Figure 4.2 shows, high achievement amongst NEET young people is more than half as common as low achievement, with the average NEET young person having modest, but not negligible, attainment.

Self, family and neighbourhood

As already noted, being NEET is just one dimension of wider experiences of social exclusion stemming from social disadvantage and deprivation, which include disrupted family relationships and the breakdown of traditional households, often leading to homelessness, crime and disaffection. Contingent factors, including major personal and family traumas, are often associated with young people becoming NEET (Finlay et al, 2010; Russell et al, 2011). In the South Glamorgan study, 'by far the majority of young people interviewed had experienced what might be called 'fractured' childhoods' (Rees et al, 1996:224), and more recent work indicates that NEET young people aged 16 and 17 are more likely to live with lone parents and to live in a household where no-one is working (Barham et al, 2009). Reporting on Australian research, Savelsberg and Martin-Giles (2008) found strong correlations between the breakdown of family relationships and precarious engagement with schooling and the labour market.

Whilst unstable family circumstances are significant, they are closely linked with poverty and unemployment, and are therefore to be expected amongst many NEET young people without necessarily being causally implicated in their NEET status. Nevertheless, in certain circumstances, events such as parental break-up or unemployment, relocation and bullying appear to overwhelm the material and cultural resources of families and individuals, precipitating drop-out from school or college or resulting in the loss of a job. The case of Shannon, a young woman in our research, illustrates the contingent yet structurally framed nature of events leading to withdrawal and underachievement. Shannon left home aged 15 due to family difficulties, and ceased attending school:

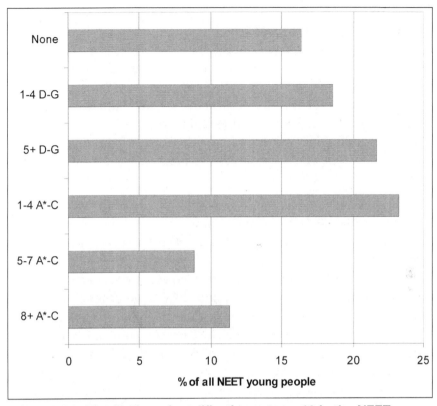

Figure 4.2: Distribution of qualifications at age 16 in the NEET population in England, 2008 Derived from DCSF/ONS (2009:30).

> I moved out when I was in Year 11. I went back for my GCSEs but I only had, like, four or five months in Year 11. I got a grade D in maths, science and English ... I was predicted B but with everything that was going on I missed a lot of revision ... I just got kicked out because me mum and me didn't get on. At the time I didn't like [school] but now I'm thinking that it was OK. I didn't like the teachers at the time because I just thought they were boring. [I wish now] that I'd worked.

Parental break-up followed by relocation was a factor in school failure for several of our participants, including Ellie – who attempted to work alone at home after dropping out of a new school that she found chaotic – and Luke, whose frequent family moves following the departure of his father to live overseas had prevented him from settling in at any school in Year 10.

Although good careers advice and a sense of direction for the future are generally accepted to be an important element of post-16 progression, there has been little research on the connection between early uncertainty or misalignment in occupational aspirations and becoming NEET between the ages of 16 and 18. However, recent work based on BCS70 indicates that this is a significant factor. Not only are uncertainty about career or educational choices and misalignment between qualifications and aspirations associated with increased risk of becoming NEET by 18, both are more widespread amongst those from poorer backgrounds (Yates *et al*, 2010).

In some deprived areas, social networks are very closely-knit, with various friends and family members from different generations all living in the same few streets (MacDonald *et al*, 2005; Green and White, 2008). Although they can provide a range of support systems, such networks may act as a constraint, reducing ambition and discouraging young people from taking up education and training opportunities. Neighbourhood and family play a significant role in specific decisions about post-16 participation. Green and White (2008) describe young people in deprived communities as highly dependent on family and friends for advice on education, training and the labour market, with official sources such as colleges, training providers and Connexions being considered less likely to give truthful information on the reality of jobs and courses. However, this situation is reversed for some ethnic minority communities, who appear to be more reliant on official sources rather than friends and families (Beck *et al*, 2006). For such reasons, as well as the constraints provided by travel costs, objective geographies of opportunity are particularly important for young people in such circumstances.

Educational disaffection

Educational disadvantage refers to inequalities due to individual attributes or to social and family circumstances; *disaffection* concerns the attitudes of young people towards education. Since the mid-1990s, research has consistently highlighted associations between educational disaffection and becoming NEET. Wilkinson (1995) and Rees *et al* (1996) found that, in general, education was not valued and training schemes were viewed with suspicion by many NEET young people. Disrupted school careers arising from truancy and school exclusion continue to be substantial risk factors, with 34 per cent of those permanently excluded from school and 28 per cent of persistent truants being NEET at age 17 (DCSF/ONS, 2009).

However, these forms of disaffection do not necessarily imply a wilful rejection of education. Both truancy and exclusion are strongly associated with schools serving deprived communities. Children receiving free school meals, looked-after children, certain ethnic minority groups and children with special educational needs are consistently over-represented in school exclusions (Munn and Lloyd, 2005). Coles *et al* (2002) report dramatic impact on the local ethnic monitoring initiatives have had on reducing exclusion rates amongst Black Caribbean boys, but this group is nonetheless still excluded at three times the rate of their white peers (Archer *et al*, 2010). Chinese and Indian students are often seen as models of high achievement, whilst other groups – particularly Black Caribbean young people and white working-class boys – are generally constructed through discourses of failure and low aspiration.

The promotion of competition between education providers and the publication of achievement league tables has led to schools becoming more reluctant to engage with young people with a history of under-achievement, truancy and school exclusion. In some cases, poor quality provision for these pupils, in preference to those closer to achieving good grades, can further reinforce disaffection (Shildrick and Mac-Donald, 2007). Provision in out-of-school contexts for pupils excluded from school is increasing; Thomson and Russell (2009) highlight the prevalence of discourses which construct these young people as a homogenous group, whose non-academic disposition makes them un-suited to conventional schooling. In our E2E research, a number of learners had truanted or experienced school exclusion, and some were already familiar with E2E providers from their experiences in alternative provision. Although these young people were often without qualifications or had underachieved in other ways, the reasons for their exclusion were varied: not all of them could be regarded as lacking in academic ability. The circumstances underlying their exclusion varied, were often contingent and did not necessarily imply disconnection from an ethos of learning:

I hated it – I didn't really go to school. I liked the classes but ... Every time I went I just got chucked back out so they sent me to Middlebridge College to do a Pathfinder [alternative provision] course for a year. I left in Year 10 and I did Pathfinder in Year 11. I didn't get any GCSEs or anything from Pathfinder. (Jessica, age 17, *Aim for Work*)

I liked Year 7 and that were brilliant but when it got to Year 9 I didn't really like it. It were alright but everyone used to mess around in the classroom and the teachers were always shouting at you and you ended up just having an argument. In Year 10 I got my predictions for GCSEs and they were for A* and a B in English but for personal reasons I stopped going to school. I would have got good GCSEs and I were proper enthusiastic as well. I did some coursework though and I got a grade A for that. (Emma, age 17, Middlebridge College [quoted in Russell *et al*, 2011])

Although a focus on disaffection helps to draw attention to the ways in which some individuals and communities become disconnected from mainstream society, the resulting discourses tend to locate responsibility for social exclusion with the excluded. As James and Simmons (2007) point out, such discourses construct negative attitudes to education, work and society as inherent characteristics of disaffected individuals, rather than understanding them in relation to a complex network of causes and circumstances. In particular, disaffection normalises middle-class relationships with schooling, presenting educational success and congruence between the values of home and school as a natural state of affairs, independent of the circumstances in which young people grow up and their differentiated experiences in terms of factors such as ethnicity, gender, disability and social class. Normative discourses of school as a place of compliance and academic success are combined with pressures to segregate middle-class children from those perceived as rejecting and challenging this ethos, for example, through ability streaming or school choices. For young people in these circumstances, educational success can be a story of pain and difficulty (Reay, 2002). It cannot be assumed that educational *affection* is a natural state; disaffection, far from being an irrational rejection of an obvious personal good, is something requiring hard work to avoid – to suggest otherwise is, as Bourdieu (1974:32) writes of educational success, to misrecognise a social gift for a natural one.

Consequences of being NEET

The diverse nature of the NEET group means that immediate reasons for non-participation are varied, and in some cases – for example, young people taking time out between school and higher education or those suffering from a short-term illness – NEET status is unlikely to have negative consequences in later life. However, this is not the case for NEET young people in general and concern about the long-term impact of non-participation has led to the intensive policy focus on this group in recent years. Those who are NEET at age 16 are considerably more likely to be in this category at 21, even when qualifications and family background are taken into account. They are also less likely to be in full-time or part-time employment at age 21. Low-attaining young people who become NEET generally experience greater difficulty in re-engaging with learning or employment than 16 to 24-year-olds, and there is evidence that they may become socially excluded on a more permanent basis.

Such exclusion is likely to prove costly, not only for the young people concerned but also for society more broadly. There is considerable international evidence for the negative impact of unemployment and disengagement from education, with a number of serious effects being reported (Bell and Blanchflower, 2010). These range from economic impacts such as recurrent unemployment and lowered future wages to emotional consequences, including anxiety, feelings of shame and rejection, and a greater likelihood of drug dependency or criminal activity. Scarpetta *et al* (2010) discuss the potentially 'scarring' effects of early youth unemployment, which include an increased likelihood of unemployment and reduced earnings in the future. For most young people, the substantial effects of early unemployment have been found to be temporary, but for disadvantaged youth lacking basic education, failures in their first experience of the labour market may expose them to long-lasting effects (Scarpetta *et al*, 2010:15-16).

There is also evidence that young people who are NEET between 16 and 18 are more likely than their peers to suffer poor health and depression (Coles *et al*, 2002). For girls in particular, being NEET at age 16 has consequences which extend beyond education and the labour market, including early motherhood and emotional problems (Bynner and Parsons, 2002). Godfrey *et al* (2002) estimate the social and public finance implications of being NEET to be significant, involving costs associated with educational underachievement, unemployment, inactivity, crime and health. They conclude that the 157,000 young people aged 16-18 who were NEET in the UK in 1999 will require £8.1 billion of additional public spending (in 2001 prices) over a lifetime, or approximately £52,000 per head. Because their study did not take into account the effect of lower skills on economic output, these figures are likely to underestimate the scale of the problem.

The UK and many other Anglophone nations have chosen to embrace globalisation through the adoption of neo-liberalism but others have contested this model. The Nordic countries, for example, have chosen to mediate its effects through encouraging greater continuity in employment and welfare than in either the UK or the USA (Lauder *et al*, 2006:46-7). Although being outside education and the labour market has negative consequences in all nations, there is some evidence to suggest that differences between countries in welfare systems and the ways in which they approach employment policy can modify significantly the long-term effects of inactivity at an early age (Furlong and Cartmel, 2003). However, the case of Sweden in the 1990s shows that even relatively generous support systems and extensive labour-market intervention cannot prevent experiences of social exclusion in young adulthood being associated with increased risk of inactivity in later years (Franzen and Kassman, 2005).

Constructing a problem category: the discourse of NEET

Policy on NEET young people in the UK implicitly distinguishes between two forms of social participation. The first – primarily paid work and education or training – is privileged and provides a focus for interventions aimed at encouraging young people to gain knowledge, skills and experience in approved ways. The second includes activities which are positioned as being of lesser value. Although occupations such as unpaid domestic labour or other unskilled work are in general socially acceptable, in the context of young people they are regarded as problematic and likely to increase the risk of future social exclusion.

This distinction is not without merit; however, it overlooks inequalities within education, work and society, combining groups of young people with very different characteristics whilst splitting disadvantaged groups on the basis of a participation status that may not be the most significant aspect of their circumstances. Consequently, the use of NEET to describe and understand young people has been the subject of sustained critique from various authors, who draw attention to its shortcomings as an instrument of policy and to the pernicious effects of a discourse which casts many young people as members of an incipient underclass. This section examines the advantages and disadvantages of using NEET to think about young people and frame policy directed towards them.

On the positive side, the NEET category has helped to maintain vulnerable young people in the policy foreground throughout a period when media images of young people celebrating yet another set of record A-level results have tended to obscure the other side of the picture. NEET status encourages a focus on youth unemployment and draws attention to contrasts between advantaged and disadvantaged young people (Furlong, 2006). It also highlights young people in difficult social or physical circumstances, such as teenage mothers and other young carers, or people with disabilities. These circumstances often lead to isolation and although, particularly for young parents, being NEET should not automatically be viewed as a negative condition, it can be a precursor to disengagement or exclusion (Yates and Payne, 2006).

Under successive New Labour governments, the policy focus on reducing NEET rates led to initiatives which contained elements of a redistributive approach to social exclusion. Measures such as EMA and the Activity Agreement pilots were not merely incentives to staying on (or 'bribes', as some young people have described the EMA); they also recognised, in however limited a way, that poverty and dropping out of education are closely related.

Using NEET to conceptualise problematic transitions may therefore benefit some young people, particularly those who are vulnerable to particular forms of social exclusion. However, it also has a number of disadvantages. Replacing unemployment with a category combining groups of young people with diverse characteristics reduces opportunities for comparison between nations and creates problems of definition and enumeration, with both cross-sectional and longitudinal approaches to capturing the size of the NEET population suffering from unreliable and incomplete data. Furlong (2006) argues that, for policy to be effective, the most vulnerable groups need to be disaggregated from those who are likely to re-engage with education or training with minimal intervention.

Focusing on overall NEET rates, particularly in the context of performance targets for agencies such as Connexions and training providers, can lead to those who are easiest to re-engage receiving the most attention and diverting resources from those who are more disadvantaged. In any case, for the most vulnerable young people, being NEET may be of secondary concern, and assistance with extreme circumstances such as homelessness or drug misuse may be more urgently required (Yates and Payne, 2006). For such young people, attention to their NEET status risks distracting attention from the more immediate and threatening risks they face and providing them with inappropriate and ill-timed choices.

Perhaps the most significant adverse consequence of discourses based on the NEET category is that they concentrate on the boundary between participation and non-participation, diverting attention from inequalities within education and employment (Thompson, 2011a). At an individual level, although initially positive outcomes such as enrolment on a college course or finding employment may be desirable in the short term, a focus on reducing NEET rates removes the need to question the longer-term prospects they provide. Roberts (2009a) argues that for many young people, post-16 education and training is merely an opportunity to achieve qualifications whose labour-market value is negligible (see also Chapter 2). Although churning between being NEET and education or employment is a fairly clear indication of disadvantage, stable post-16 participation can also be part of young people's experience of social exclusion. Fergusson (2004) identifies a new form of educational inequality, in which the continued participation of some young people arises from a lack of alternative opportunities. This form of inequality has not been a priority within approaches to monitoring social exclusion amongst young people in the UK.

Cultures of worklessness?

Political debate on NEET young people slides all too often into the moral underclass discourse of social exclusion. This discourse constructs certain groups of people – such as the long-term unemployed – as being afflicted by a deep-seated malaise endemic to their families and communities. The notion of a moral underclass has, if anything, been intensified in Coalition policies on welfare, employment and education. In their Foreword to the education White Paper of 2010, the Prime Minister and Deputy Prime Minister write in disapproving terms that 'In far too many communities there is a deeply embedded culture of low aspiration that is strongly tied to long-term unemployment' (DfE, 2010b:4). This image of recalcitrant individuals disconnected from education, work and society is reiterated by the Secretary of State for Work and Pensions:

> As I travelled to many of Britain's poorest communities I concluded that tackling poverty had to be about much more than handing out money. It was bigger than that. *I could see we were dealing with a part of society that had become detached from the rest of us.* People who suffer high levels of family breakdown, educational failure, personal debt, addiction – *and at the heart of all of this is intergenerational worklessness.* Only in understanding this can poverty be defeated. (Duncan Smith, 2010, emphasis added)

Notions about intergenerational cultures of worklessness and benefit dependency form a central part of the moral underclass discourse and provide much of the ideology underpinning individualistic conceptions of NEET policy. Ever since this discourse emerged in the 1980s (Byrne, 2005:24), the idea of an underclass has attracted extensive critique. Wilson and Wacquant (1989) argue that apparent underclass behaviours can be explained in terms of structural factors within the economy and society, for example through the concentration of economically marginal individuals within neighbourhoods cheap enough to be accessible to them. It is also important to distinguish having no work from wanting no work. Although *Bridging the Gap* (SEU, 1999:48) identifies 'being from a family with little or no history of work (sometimes back to the third generation)' as a major contributor to the chances of becoming NEET, it links this factor with experiencing pressures to leave education to contribute to family income. In this context, Finlay *et al* (2010) make the important distinction between low *aspirations* and low *expectations*, arguing that the latter is based on empirical observation by socially excluded young people of the opportunities and outcomes experienced by others like them.

Numerous empirical studies have attempted to locate an underclass and uncover the cultures of worklessness associated with it, largely without success (although poverty and disadvantage are somewhat easier to find). Rees *et al* (1996) concluded that although some NEET young people were likely to resist interventions there was no evidence that they formed part of an underclass, and argued for increased state investment in education and training to benefit the majority. More recent studies found the underclass to be equally elusive (Macdonald and Marsh, 2001; McKendrick *et al,* 2007). In a deprived area of Glasgow, McKendrick *et al* found no evidence for widespread disaffection or disengagement, or for a distinct sub-group of the most problematic individuals. Indeed, contrary to the underclass discourse, Shildrick and MacDonald (2007) point to a hyper-conventional work ethic amongst socially excluded young people, in which any work takes precedence over deferred – and dubious – labour market returns from education and training. Murad (2002) describes similar class-based orientations to work amongst socially-excluded groups in Europe as remarkably persistent. For Macdonald and Marsh, the economic and social marginality of disadvantaged young people in Teesside resulted from the restructuring of employment in post-industrial, flexible labour markets. Significantly, they found that being socially excluded in itself attracted a general stigma which affected job prospects.

NEET and the dynamics of social exclusion

The importance attached by successive UK governments to reducing NEET rates can be understood through social integrationist as well as underclass discourses of social exclusion. Discourses of social integration construct work as a moral and social good, and promote images of an organic society characterised by solidarity and interdependence. In the context of education, they portray lifelong learning – the continuing acquisition of skills and qualifications – as the pathway to inclusion and social mobility, enabling individuals to improve their position in employment markets and contributing to wealth creation for the benefit of all.

However, such discourses are flawed in two ways. Firstly, they construct educational achievement and social mobility as equivalent, assuming that employment growth will keep pace with educational expansion, in spite of considerable evidence to the contrary (see Chapter 2). Secondly, they leave unexamined the outcomes for those who do not achieve the desired upward mobility, representing poor work and unemployment as the inevitable penalty for individual failings. As Levitas (2005) points out, the social integrationist discourse obscures inequalities within paid employment and disregards the exploitation inherent to capitalist modes of production.

Steinert (2003) refers to a *horizontal* conception of social exclusion, in which the powerful and privileged disappear within an included majority. Levitas draws attention to the inadequacy of this conception: 'The solution implied by a discourse of social exclusion is a minimalist one: a transition across the boundary to become an insider rather than an outsider in a society whose structural inequalities remain largely un-interrogated' (Levitas, 2005:7).

The relational nature of social mobility, as a process in which some make progress but others are left behind, thereby contributing to social exclusion, is woven out of the discourse. Fairclough (2000) argues that New Labour used social exclusion more often to describe a condition that people are in than to describe a process in which something is done to them; Veit-Wilson (1998) distinguishes between weak and strong conceptualisations of social exclusion:

> In the 'weak' version of this discourse, the solutions lie in altering these excluded people's handicapping characteristics and enhancing their integration into dominant society. 'Stronger' forms of this discourse also emphasise the role of those who are doing the excluding and therefore aim for solutions which reduce the powers of exclusion. (Veit-Wilson, 1998:45)

Giddens (1998) proposes that middle-class self-exclusion from public services is a significant factor in social exclusion generally. Whitty (2001) applies this argument to education, emphasising that exclusion of middle class cultural and social capital from areas of state schooling deemed unsafe or inadequate for more privileged children contributes to the social exclusion of poorer families. Middle-class self-exclusion from certain schools is not merely an absence: it can have both subjective and objective consequences, demonising neighbourhoods and schools and depriving them of social and cultural capital. The outcome is a set of practices and discourses which act to exclude poor families from more successful schools and construct whole swathes of state education as 'places on the margins' (Reay and Lucey, 2004; Reay, 2007). Whilst, for middle-class families, these discourses may legitimate their avoidance of such places, the children who end up actually attending marginalised schools must cope with the consequences.

> My school wasn't even like a school. It was more like a playground for the first four years because the headteacher was just rubbish ... I got to Year 11 and then a new headteacher came and everything changed and then everybody was getting kicked out. [I got excluded for] poor attendance – like being late and stuff. They didn't put me in at all [for GCSEs]. (Leon, age 16, Middle-bridge College)

Although working-class children may construct counter-narratives which represent their schools by more positive images, the remaining message is that good schools, and by implication successful students, are located elsewhere. By valorising exclusionary strategies as the exercise of choice, and attributing educational failure to deficits acquired in family, community and school, policies based on weak versions of social exclusion overlook its dynamic nature, as a process involving social practices which maintain or deepen inequality. Perhaps the central weakness of the NEET category as a way of thinking about socially excluded young people is that it largely fails to contest such processes, weaving them instead into a horizontal discourse of inclusion and opportunity.

Supporting to learn and paying to learn: Connexions and EMA

Connexions

One of the first actions of the Labour government elected in 1997 was to establish the Social Exclusion Unit, with a brief to review various dimensions of social exclusion; the report on NEET young people, *Bridging the Gap* (SEU, 1999) was one of the outcomes. An important conclusion was the variable quality of careers advice and other support for young people, and a number of weaknesses in these services were identified. These included institutional fragmentation, insufficient preparation for post-school choices and a lack of coherent support for young people once they had left school (p78). The White Paper *Learning to Succeed* (DfEE, 1999) announced the creation of a new service incorporating multi-agency working and a focus on increasing participation in education and training amongst 16 to 18-year-olds. The new service, Connexions, was phased in from 2001 to provide integrated advice and guidance for young people in England aged 13-19. This brought together holistically the operations of the former Careers Service and a range of other services, with the declared aims of helping young people access appropriate support and make a successful transition to adulthood. By 2003, Connexions was operating across England in 47 regional partnerships; a year later, its budget was approximately £450m, supporting a workforce of 7,700 Personal Advisers and over 2,400 other front line staff (Hoggarth and Smith, 2004). As a measure explicitly designed to reduce the social and financial costs of youth unemployment and social exclusion, its primary initial target was to reduce the proportion of NEET 16 to 18-year-olds by 10 per cent.

At the centre of Connexions activity is the relationship between a young person and their Personal Adviser (PA), in which openness and flexibility rather than a focus on pre-determined progression outcomes is crucial (Maguire and Thompson, 2007). These PAs are intended to liaise with other professionals in responding to the general needs of all young people, and in providing more intensive support to those seen as particularly vulnerable. Leadbeater (2004:18) argues that recent government discourse on joined-up provision and personalisation has resulted in a shift in the way education and other professionals are seen, with a decreased emphasis on expert knowledge and a re-conceptualisation of youth professionals as solution-assemblers: brokering support, advice and advocacy in order to 'relay and translate [government] strategies into action' (p24). This is certainly the case with Connexions PAs, who aim to improve outcomes for young people and influence how other services respond to them. However, as Simmons (2009:141) points out, personalisation creates educational spaces in different ways: for more advantaged groups it can assist processes of self-actualisation whereas for those on the margins, personalisation can be viewed as subsidiary to pre-assembled solutions to deficits singled out for attention as inhibiting re-engagement in work and society.

Although much valuable work was done by Connexions, from the outset a number of tensions were evident. Some of these stemmed from the organisational and historical circumstances of the service; however, perhaps the main issue – and the focus of much concern from PAs in our research – was the tension between soft outcomes relating to personal development and the underlying needs of young people, and the harder-edged regime of targets which prioritised reducing NEET rates (Yates and Payne, 2006; Russell *et al*, 2010). Formulating targets in terms of progression to education, employment or training constrained PAs to focus on this type of outcome, particularly those readily available, rather than the real needs of individual young people. The emphasis on destinations which are easily measured and related to service targets 'diverts attention and resources away from other outcomes ... *which young people may need first* in order to be able to achieve the harder outcomes' (Hoggarth and Smith, 2004:206).

Ironically, in view of the origin of Connexions in calls for a holistic approach to guidance, the Coalition government have emphasised the importance of specialist careers advice in the decisions of young people. The all-age careers service introduced in September 2011 is claimed to 'build on the best' of Connexions and the adult Next Step service (Hayes, 2010), and schools rather than local authorities will have a responsibility to commission careers advice for their students, essentially creating a market in guidance. However, local authorities still have an obligation to look after young people at risk of becoming NEET, and will continue to maintain data on the activities of young people so that support can be targeted at those in most need (*ibid*).

The Educational Maintenance Allowance

Although financial support for young people in education between the ages of 16 and 18 has a long history, the cumulative effect of benefit changes in the 1980s and 1990s was a complex landscape of support, involving eight government agencies and labyrinthine rules (SEU, 1999: 45). Prior to 1999, the primary sources of financial support for full-time students in this age group were discretionary awards from LEAs and the remission of fees; however, budgetary restrictions during the 1990s led to a fall in the number of LEAs offering discretionary awards, and between 1990 and1999 expenditure on awards to support further education fell by 10 per cent (Maguire, 2008:206). Modelled on youth allowances in Australia, EMA was intended to redress this situation, and provide clarity in the support available for study.

Pilots began in 1999, initially in fifteen LEAs in England. EMA was extended to the whole of the UK from 2004, with varying eligibility requirements in Scotland, Wales and Northern Ireland. Although a higher level of payment had been made in some of the pilots, the national EMA comprised a weekly payment of up to £30, made directly to young people from low-income households who were following education or training courses involving at least twelve hours of guided learning per week. A system of termly bonuses was available to young people meeting agreed targets. As Maguire (2008) points out, EMA was a tacit acceptance that paying young people to learn may be necessary to achieve government aspirations on participation. However, its effectiveness was constantly under scrutiny and from December 2010, EMA was terminated in England by the Coalition government, with the stated intention of replacing it with allowances targeted at those in most need. In Scotland, allowances have been reduced, and in Northern Ireland EMA is under review.

To some extent, being paid to learn is appreciated by many young people, although some regard it as a bribe or part of official measures to coerce them into education (Archer *et al*, 2010:117). These mixed feelings were also evident in our E2E research, where although considerable scepticism existed, the frequent delays and problems with payments appeared to cause frustration and sometimes hardship.

> I only started getting paid, like, three weeks ago. £30 a week is not a lot but it does [help]. That's why I like getting up because I'm getting paid for it ... [because of] the money. It sounds horrible, but yeah ... [Without EMA], if the placement hadn't have been so good I might not have stayed but with it being so good then I am doing it and I haven't been late once. (Jade, *MGC Training*)

The aspect of coercion was resented by some, who saw EMA sanctions as disproportionate: 'Like if you do one thing then that's all your money gone ... and you've still got to come in for the rest of the week knowing that you are not going to get the money' (Donna, *MGC Training*). Reliability, and the low level of incentive provided compared with training schemes such as YTS, were highlighted by practitioners, although some saw EMA – as opposed to a training allowance – as a possible disincentive to taking up work placements.

> We've had some lads who've been here since July and didn't get EMA until September. For them to stay seven or eight weeks without any money was

pretty remarkable and we've still got some who haven't got their EMA sorted out and a few have left because of it. A lot of them still borrow money off their parents and if I go back to when I left school – in '82 – and I started on my placement I got £75 a week. So what they get now is nothing, is it? (George, *Action for Youth*)

There's no incentive for them now [because they get the same whether they're here or out on placement] ... It depends how you look at it: technically, EMA is just to get them to their place of learning and it's not, in effect, a wage ... We try to teach them the world of work or whatever and the EMA system seems to be against it. They've all got friends who are working and earning £150 a week and they are only getting £30 a week. (John, *Action for Youth*)

There is some evidence to suggest that EMA increased participation rates and, in a limited way, assisted lower-attaining young people to achieve slightly higher levels of qualification than hitherto. However, the effectiveness of EMA in increasing participation was less than might be hoped, with one study reporting that only 12 per cent of those receiving the allowance believing that they would not have participated in the courses they were taking had it not been available to them (NFER, 2010: 54). In view of the limited impact on labour market fortunes discussed in Chapter 2, this was unlikely to decrease social inequality. Maguire (2008:212) notes that the lack of impact on achievement 'raises alarm bells about young people being warehoused in education, as opposed to providing young people with the opportunity to make progress, in terms of qualification enhancement'.

Possibly the most contentious aspect of EMA was its value for money. Like many other benefits, it carries a considerable dead-weight cost: for example, child benefit aims to alleviate child poverty but is made widely available to avoid low uptakes which may result from means testing. This involves a considerable cost in payments to relatively well-off families. Similarly, EMA was paid to many young people who would have stayed in education without it. Indeed, its high take-up made it expensive; in the last full year of its operation, EMA cost £560m in payments (NFER, 2010). Such considerations were used by the incoming Coalition government as part of their justification for terminating EMA, and targeting more limited funding at those most in need. This suggestion was supported by findings in the NFER study concerning the greater weight given to financial constraints by those who were NEET, were in jobs with no training, or had learning difficulties or disabilities. However, targeted support aimed at re-integrating NEET young people back into learning has had mixed success. The pilots of Activity Agreements, which operated from 2006, had a number of positive effects, but faced problems of uptake and conflicts with benefit rules: the most vulnerable and most in need appeared to be particularly hard to reach (Maguire *et al*, 2009).

This evidence should not be taken to imply that financial support for participation in education or training makes no difference to young people. Apart from limitations in the sample, which contained many young people at a very early stage in their studies and was not representative of the 16-18 age group as a whole, other findings in the NFER study indicate that the impact of EMA may be more subtle than through raw participation rates. In particular, 18 per cent reported that they would have done a different course – presumably one they preferred – had they received more money to cover aspects such as transport, books and food. Furthermore, 15 per cent of those with part-time work said that their job enabled them to continue in learning, suggesting that financial support may help students make more use of study time.

In March 2011, the Coalition government announced that £180m would be available annually in England for more targeted allowances to replace EMA. £15m of this will be used to give 12,000 of the most disadvantaged 16 to 19-year-olds bursaries of £1,200 per year. The remainder will expand the existing £26m of discretionary funding distributed through schools, colleges and other providers to help their poorest students with the costs of study; providers may make these payments conditional on attendance and behaviour. Although some aspects of these proposals may help to alleviate specific problems associated with EMA, there has been a shift in how support for learners is conceptualised. Whilst protecting some of those in extreme need, these measures may overlook other vulnerable young people and highlight the privileging of certain forms of state subsidy for young people and their families – for example, charitable status for independent schools – over support for the poorest members of society.

5

Entry to Employment: Young People, Learning and Agency

arlier chapters explored the relationship between knowledge, economy and learning and its impact on the opportunities available to marginalised young people. We have shown how social and economic structures can limit the exercise of agency and have questioned the traditional liberal image of education as an un-diluted benefit for young people, which it is irrational of them to reject. As we have seen, some propose that education is not about equality but about inequality: 'Education's main purpose of the social integration of a class society could be achieved only by preparing most kids for an unequal future, and by ensuring their personal underdevelopment' (Willis, 1983: 110).

Whilst we broadly support this position, the question of individual agency and the relative autonomy of educational institutions cannot be ignored. Schools, colleges and training providers do not simply repro-duce orientations towards work and study, placing young people into pre-assigned roles. Nor do individual learners meekly submit to lives of low-paid, insecure work. Educational institutions are social sites characterised by cultures and ideologies that are partly independent of government priorities. In E2E, the complexity and contradictions of educational institutions and their relationship with the economy and society are particularly apparent.

This chapter examines the nature and content of E2E provision, beginning with the origins of the programme and its roots in the earlier youth training and life skills programmes discussed in Chapter 3. The remainder of the chapter centres on the lived experience of young people undertaking E2E programmes, drawing on ethnographic data collected in the four learning sites introduced in Chapter 1. We attempt to provide insights into the diversity, contradictions and contestation which permeate such institutions, through the experiences of the learners and teachers who inhabit them. Important themes emerging from the data are explored:

- the young people's orientations to work and study and how they came to access E2E

- their future ambitions and likely prospects in the knowledge economy

- the nature of teaching and learning in the case-study sites

- the ways in which agency, culture and structural constraints influenced young people's engagement with the programme.

E2E: origins and curriculum structure

As we saw in Chapter 3, youth training schemes became increasingly discredited through a lack of employers offering training which could lead to secure employment, and the expansion of full-time education as an alternative to work-based learning. By 2001, when the Secretary of State for Education and Employment announced a reform of the Modern Apprenticeship scheme introduced by the Conservative government in 1994, all that remained was some Life Skills work and the ambiguously labelled *Other Training* – 'the residue of the old, failed Youth Training programmes' (Blunkett, 2001, para. 52).

The subsequent Cassels Report (DfES, 2001) identified a continuing need for courses aimed at young people considered not ready to enter employment, an apprenticeship, or other forms of further education and training. It proposed a new work-based learning pathway to support these young people, who were characterised as having 'low levels of prior attainment, social or behavioural problems which stand in the way of sustained participation, or limitations on their innate ability' (p27). The new pathway, Entry to Employment, was conceived largely as pre-apprenticeship provision, although it was anticipated that some participants may not be suited to an apprenticeship, and in such cases a more limited aim of settled employment was recognised.

The Cassels Report recommended that participation in E2E should be possible only on referral by Connexions, so would include only young people with barriers to participation. This led to restrictions on the target group, which comprised mainly unemployed young people aged 16 to 18 (on the day they started E2E) who were not ready to enter structured learning leading to a Level 2 qualification. With the agreement of the Learning and Skills Council, certain people aged 19 to 24 – for example those with learning difficulties – and some who were employed, could also be eligible (LSDA, 2003). Young people attending E2E programmes formed a very diverse group, who had a wider range of abilities, aspirations and circumstances than was at first evident from the target group. Furthermore, in spite of clear recommendations in the Cassels Report that funding mechanisms should not encourage providers to maximise learner numbers, programme evaluations indicated that referrals to E2E had exceeded expectations and included some young people, such as those with severe learning difficulties, for whom it was seen as inappropriate. This was partly because of a lack of alternatives for vulnerable young people; however, some providers appeared to have an admissions policy aimed at generating income rather than strictly applying the national eligibility criteria (Tusting and Barton, 2007).

Although publicly funded, E2E was delivered by a range of public, private and voluntary sector organisations, which were expected to have expertise in working with young people in challenging circumstances. Providers were required to work in partnership with Connexions and other local agencies able to give specialised help to young people with specific problems and foster links with local employers, particularly those willing to provide opportunities for young people who had experienced difficulty in finding and retaining employment (Simmons, 2009).

Significantly, E2E was regarded largely as a transitional programme, intended to move young people on relatively quickly. It was therefore not conceived as a fixed-term course with a specific syllabus or qualification aims. This approach allowed a degree of personalisation and flexibility, encouraging providers to take a broader view of learners' development and – as with earlier programmes such as YOP (Gleeson, 1989) – injecting progressive elements of education into largely instrumental provision. But it contained a fundamental flaw. Although in principle E2E was not time-bound, pressure on providers to demonstrate quality through progression outcomes, together with limitations on learner numbers, meant that in practice it could be difficult to retain young people for enough time to make real differences to their employability or ability to benefit from further study (Russell *et al*, 2010).

E2E commenced in 2002 with a pilot phase involving eleven partnerships across England and in 2003 was extended to the whole country. Table 5.1 compares the size of the E2E cohort with participation in other post-16 learning, including full-time education and work-based learning. Although learner numbers at any time tend to be relatively low, the high turnover means that total participation is significantly higher. In November 2008, when our research began, 21,500 E2E learners aged 16-18 were enrolled and during 2008-09 a total of 78,100 learners embarked on E2E programmes (Russell *et al*, 2011). As Table 5.1 shows, male learners tend to predominate in E2E (and in work-based learning more generally), accounting for approximately 60 per cent of participants in 2008-09, whereas in full-time education there is a small majority of female participants in the 16-18 age group.

Thousands

	2008			2009		
	Female	Male	All	Female	Male	All
FT Ed	670.2	635.5	1,305.7	690.7	673.9	1,364.6
WBL	49.8	83.7	133.5	49.6	75.5	125.1
E2E	8.4	13.1	21.5	8.4	13.2	21.6
NEET	94.4	115.7	210.1	80.6	109.1	189.7
All 16-18 year olds	982.9	1040.8	2,023.6	967.8	1024.2	1,992.0

Table 5.1: 16-18 learner numbers (in thousands) on LSC-funded provision in full-time education (FT Ed), all work-based learning (WBL) and E2E for 2008 and 2009 Source: SFR18 Supplementary Tables C13-15 (2010)

The E2E curriculum

Although there was no common syllabus or standard set of qualification aims, E2E programmes were required to provide learning opportunities in three core areas: personal and social development, basic skills, and vocational development (LSC, 2006). This structure is continued in the Foundation Learning programmes which absorbed E2E in late 2010. Learning was intended to meet the individual needs of each young person, and to reflect their stage of development. For example, learners with complex personal circumstances or specific developmental problems may not be regarded as able to benefit from vocational learning until these factors had begun to be addressed. Although E2E had no fixed length in terms of programme duration, most learners attended for between 16 and 40 hours per week over a 22-week period.

Work placements or experience in simulated work environments, vocational tasters and other work-related activities were intended to form an important part of the learning opportunities provided for young people. In addition, optional work-related learning in specialised vocational areas and preparation for Level 2 learning opportunities could be provided. E2E had four broad learning objectives: learners should increase their motivation and confidence, develop basic and key skills, improve personal effectiveness, and acquire vocational knowledge, skills and understanding (LSDA, 2003). Progress was closely monitored, and those who appeared to be unsuited to the programme, for example because of poor attendance, uncooperative behaviour or personal problems – could be referred back to Connexions.

As we saw earlier, the structure of work-based learning programmes such as E2E attributes high levels of youth unemployment primarily to the shortcomings of young people and the ineffectiveness of mainstream education in providing them with the skills required by employers (Simmons, 2009). Social integrationist and moral underclass discourses of social exclusion are intertwined, with an emphasis on deficiencies in personal capital. Thus E2E learners are not merely to be equipped with work-related skills; they are to be re-shaped as individuals and given a different outlook on life.

This therapeutic approach to education is becoming widespread and leads to a focus on the self as the object of study and renewal (Ecclestone and Hayes, 2008). It is hardly surprising that programmes such as E2E incorporate therapeutic elements, in which individual dispositions are closely monitored and treated as barriers to learning which must be overcome. However, we found little evidence of an excessive focus on psychological traits and behaviours and in our research this re-formation of the self took place within and alongside the development of vocational knowledge and skills. In any case, particularly for vulnerable young people, the judicious pursuit of therapeutic outcomes may be associated with educationally worthwhile goals (Hyland, 2009).

Of greater concern may be the nature of vocational knowledge itself, in terms of the content of work-based learning for marginalised young people. Such courses are work-based, not in the sense of being embedded in the learner's own employment, but by using work-related activities to provide a context which, it is assumed, will increase motivation and provide meaning through its credibility and relevance to the world of work. Thus, aspects of socialisation, basic general education, and vocationally-related skills are brought together and re-contextualised in a synthetic workplace which, however credibly it simulates real experiences of work and life, lacks the permanence and authenticity normally associated with decent jobs.

To understand the limitations of this approach, it is useful to draw on the work of Basil Bernstein on how knowledge is selected, contextualised and distributed through educational practices and discourse. His framework is used by a number of authors to analyse the nature of work-based curricula. Gleeson (1989) draws attention to the forms of knowledge made available to young people taking part in YOP and early YTS programmes, arguing that lower-level vocational courses are often taught uncritically and do not confront the inequality that so strongly influences the lived experience of learners.

More recently, Simmons (2009) uses Bernstein's work to evaluate the specific nature of the E2E curriculum. Bernstein identifies a generic mode of pedagogic discourse in which skills seen as transferable are extracted from their original vocational contexts and brought together under abstract headings such as employability or learning skills. Bernstein points out that such skills are often taught in isolation from the social practices in which they originate. However, he also provides an analysis which contrasts the knowledge acquired through generic modes with the greater power of knowledge structures based on principles and concepts at a high level of abstraction to describe and analyse situations. These *vertical discourses* (Bernstein, 2000) are associated with high-status learning, including traditional academic subjects and higher professional training, such as medicine and architecture. By contrast, in programmes such as E2E, the close association between the forms of knowledge they promote (in Bernstein's terminology, *horizontal discourses*) and specific material circumstances limit their effectiveness, their range of application, and – crucially – their status.

E2E providers and selection of the case-study sites

E2E programmes in Middlebridge and Greenford operated as a partnership, led by an FE college and involving organisations from both local authorities. The partnership comprised twenty providers drawn from the public, private and voluntary sectors; at the beginning of our research, 674 young people were enrolled on E2E. A cross-partnership unit based at Middlebridge College, the lead provider, was responsible for monitoring quality and co-ordinating activities, including staff training events. A proportion of funding was taken from the partnership's overall income to support these functions, and provide enrichment activities for young people that could be accessed by individual providers. The partnership appeared to be successful, with completion and progression rates at or above the expectations for E2E nationally, and managers felt that it compared favourably with others in the region.

Initial data on fifteen of the twenty providers were reviewed as described in Chapter 1, to help us assess the character of provision across the partnership and select suitable case-study sites for more detailed analysis. In spite of considerable diversity amongst these providers, they shared many common features in which the aims and structure of E2E were apparent. The following field note extracts give some flavour of this initial survey; the first is from a voluntary-sector provider which later became one of our sites, whilst the second is from a private-sector organisation which was not selected.

Action for Youth

Action for Youth, a charity established in 1979, is based in an old mill and rents the buildings from a landowner. They have been in these premises for just over ten years and offer engineering, construction and motor vehicle courses – learners may do all three if they wish. *Action for Youth* currently have 77 young people enrolled. They sometimes do work for Social Services, like gardening for the disabled or elderly.

The motor vehicle course uses a garage, built for this purpose behind the offices. Cars are bought from auction, repaired to MOT standard then returned to auction. Young people learn how to change a tyre and do bodywork repairs. In engineering, they learn welding and have worked on security grilles and gates. Gillian [provider manager] says they'll have a go at anything and occasionally do small jobs for outside firms; they have done some work for the camping industry. Materials are recycled where possible – she shows me a sculpture of a hand, made by a learner from nails and car bits. Building maintenance covers anything construction related, including plastering, plumbing, brickwork, coving or even changing a plug.

As well as vocational training, *Action for Youth* offer courses such as first aid, manual handling, drug awareness, sexual health and equal opportunities. A group are [away] at the moment doing an abrasive wheel course. Outdoor activities are also offered – young people are taken potholing, canoeing and do an overnight residential in a bunkhouse in the Dales, all of which are free. They also have a free canteen serving bacon butties, and sandwiches at lunch time. Young people may learn to cook basic meals there, as some live independently. *Action for Youth* have basic skills tutors who help with literacy and numeracy, although they make a point of not 'shoving this down their throat'. They do online national tests in basic skills. There is a placement officer responsible for getting young people into work experience, apprenticeships or college but sometimes the young people help using personal contacts.

They work with a difficult group who are disadvantaged, disaffected and may have been in trouble with the police. Many have social issues. They tend to retain staff, the newest joined the team eighteen months ago. The staff are all from industry, none started out as teachers, the majority are going for their Certificate in Education to keep in line with Government moves to professionalise the workforce.

Hair Training

The E2E area is entered via a working hair salon. A young man greets us at the door and rings to inform Julie that we've arrived. We walk through the salon and upstairs to an office area. Julie is busy cleaning. She is an administrator, but helps interview the young people as they start. Most referrals are from Connexions. Julie says the group they tend to work with used to be named 'underachievers' but explains that they shouldn't use that terminology nowadays. She explains that they 'look at the whole person here', using information from Connexions on the young people's personal lives as well as their qualifications. Some have GCSE grade C or above but just lack confidence. Some are dyslexic. Julie says they do a lot of counselling, and the social strand of the programme is really brought out here because they are a small, close-knit provider. Apprenticeships are offered as well as E2E.

Currently, 24 learners attend E2E. Julie says she recently interviewed four girls who cannot enrol yet as they must wait for places to become available. Some learners are on work placement in the salon downstairs. Julie says they are encouraged to get a placement as this is what builds up their confidence. It is easier to find placements just before the Christmas period. Hair Training have strong links with other salons and learners are carefully selected for appropriate work placements. Julie says it is important to place a young person in the right salon; there is usually a trial period and learners must have enough confidence to make a success of this. The dress code here is that young people must be dressed in black, silver, grey or white. If they turn up in a tracksuit they are sent home. Some young people are desperate to get a work placement, and walk around the local shopping districts to find one. The young people are encouraged to find their own placement; this is seen as part of the process.

Julie says E2E is not just about the teaching, she says 'you do become more involved'. She says she often knows what a young person is about to say before they approach her, she gives an example of a young woman saying she is pregnant, and jokes about this being quite a common occurrence. Learners are mostly girls but there are some boys. Kelly [Connexions PA] talks about one lad who transferred from *Action for Youth*. It took him a long time to build up the confidence to ask, but when he did he loved it, although he got some banter for coming here. She says young people have to be really certain about wanting this particular provision and they explore this at the interview stage.

A number of considerations influenced our final selection of case-study sites. Firstly, we wanted to include providers from the public, private and voluntary sectors, in order to highlight possible differences between these sectors and variations in learner experiences. Secondly, we wanted to examine how different vocational skills were approached by providers. Furthermore, it soon became clear that certain vocational areas tended to be associated with gendered provision, with male or female learners predominating in providers specialising in skills linked to traditional gender roles. A range of vocational areas were required to obtain a gender balance broadly representative of learner numbers nationally. Finally, providers differed to some extent in the progression strategies they used with learners, often tailoring provision to encourage progression to other courses they offered or to apprenticeships within the same organisation. Such differences were reflected in our final selection (see Table 1.1).

Young people and E2E programmes

In an early study of E2E learners, Spielhofer *et al* (2003:12-14) describe these young people as a diverse group with very different needs, and containing a significant proportion whose previous experience of education has left them with low self-esteem and mistrustful of tutors. The individual circumstances of the learners they describe place many of these young people amongst the most marginalised and vulnerable in society, comprising three overlapping categories: those who are educationally disadvantaged; young people in difficult personal circumstances; and the disengaged or socially marginal. The first category includes those with low attainment and various special needs, including dyslexia, learning difficulties or physical disabilities. The second contains young offenders and those with severe personal problems such as alcoholism, drug abuse or behavioural difficulties. The final category includes young people with disrupted educational careers, those lacking in confidence and others whose personal circumstances, such as single-parenthood or caring responsibilities, prevent them from moving on to employment or further education. Other research into E2E, such as the work of Ecclestone (2009), highlights similar characteristics, and it will be clear from Chapter 4 that E2E learners share many of the characteristics of NEET young people in general. Indeed, a significant proportion of new entrants to the NEET category come from E2E programmes.

The practitioners interviewed in our research described a range of characteristics similar to that found by Spielhofer *et al* (2003), referring to personal and developmental problems and sometimes using colourful language about sink estates or families who had 'gone off the rails'.

Although their accounts often began with the words 'They're all different', a number of common themes emerged, reflecting official discourse on E2E learners and focusing largely on deficits. As with many low-level further education programmes, referral to E2E was sometimes a result of having few alternatives, and one thing learners had in common was a lack of opportunities. However, most practitioners recognised the diversity of E2E learners and – at least in principle – emphasised the need for an individualised approach.

> You're looking at someone who, at that stage in time, doesn't want full-time education or can't access it; someone who probably doesn't have the skills necessary to enter the working market such as the ability to pass a job interview or put a CV together or present themselves. And you are looking at people who, at that stage in their education, haven't got what it takes to manage an apprenticeship. So it's more a default position. Conversely there are young people out there who ... are not ready for E2E either. So there is another step below that.

> The vast majority of [E2E learners] have underperformed in terms of education. It might not be that they haven't got their GCSEs but it might be that they just don't have the right behaviour ... A substantial number have dyslexia problems; they will have ADHD and some of the behavioural problems. They're a vulnerable group although they are extremely diverse and each has their own specific needs and E2E is meant to be an individualised programme ... There is a huge fear factor for young people when they enter the labour market, particularly for those [where] full-time education hasn't worked. They've got pretty low self-esteem even if they come across as tough and aggressive but that's just part of the armour they wear. So if the world of work doesn't want them and the world of education has already failed what else is there for them? (Careers manager)

> We've had some with seven A-C GCSEs. It could be someone who has dropped out of the sixth form because they don't like it or they've had a life crisis and they need time to readjust and there is nowhere else to go. We've got someone starting now who has had enough of sixth form after a few months and is having a change of tack. (Tutor, Middlebridge College)

Many of the young people who took part in our research had difficult lives and fitted the broad profiles described by practitioners, previous research into E2E and, indeed, much of the discourse surrounding NEET young people generally. In their own accounts, some learners corresponded closely to several of the characteristics described by Spielhofer *et al*, although there was invariably complexity and contingency not far below the surface:

> I used to go to school but then skive lessons ... Just to fit in with my friends really but I'm not friends with them now ... I moved out [of home] and I were a dosser for a couple of years and then I came here but then left because I couldn't settle. I never used to turn in and stuff. I came here and did retail and then I got kicked off the course ... There was too much stuff going on with my boyfriend and I were coming in with a black eye ... But then I came back and re-applied and did an eight week course – down the bottom of here – a fitness course. And then I came up here [to do E2E]

> I don't have close friends. It's just me, my boyfriend and my flat. I've got a lot of responsibilities really compared to the other girls who are the same age as me. They're not bothered about going out and getting drunk on the streets but I'm not interested in all that. (Ruth, *MGC Training*)

Appendix 1, which summarises some of the characteristics of the young people interviewed, indicates the serious challenges many of them faced and the educational disruption and underachievement which often resulted. Some described histories of illness, accidental injury or learning disabilities. More than half our participants had been NEET in the past, and the great majority had experienced churning between various forms of participation, including college courses, other E2E programmes or paid employment. Negative experiences of schooling were common, and many learners had not completed compulsory schooling or taken GCSE examinations. In some cases, school exclusion or systematic truancy had effectively ended their school careers at the age of 14.

The domestic circumstances of many E2E learners fitted a broad picture of deprivation and social exclusion. Nearly half our participants lived with a lone parent, compared with a quarter of all 16-17 year olds in the UK (Barham *et al*, 2009:27). Some lived independently, having various degrees of contact with their parents. A significant number faced challenging circumstances at home and in their neighbourhood, including caring responsibilities, domestic violence or involvement with youth offending. The typology of Spielhofer *et al* (2003) is well supported by our research; a significant issue, however, is whether this way of thinking about young people attending E2E programmes tells us the whole story, or is an adequate basis for practice and policy.

The experiences of Lewis, aged 17 and attending E2E at Middlebridge College, indicate the range of circumstances we encountered, although it would be mistaken to infer that these experiences are typical. Lewis had been one of a group of pupils excluded from school at the beginning of Year 11, following an incident in which a bottle was thrown from a bus window. After spending some time at home, Lewis 'got into a bit of trouble and was sent away for a bit'. Following his release from a Young Offenders' Institution, he decided to leave the area where he lived with his mother – a 'bad area' in which he felt he might re-offend – and moved in with his aunt and uncle. Whilst serving his sentence, Lewis had found out about E2E from Connexions and was able to take up a place at *Aim for Work*, one of our case-study sites. Although he spent three months at this provider, Lewis disliked what he saw as an excessively classroom-based focus and asked for a transfer. He was happy at the college and was supported in his choice by his mother. In spite of the disruption to his education, Lewis had taken GCSE examinations, although he achieved only a few grade E passes. He had some work experience in landscaping and in a warehouse. Lewis aimed to join an engineering course at Middlebridge College in the following September, and hoped for employment in this field.

Lewis's biography and the earlier quotation from Ruth's interview illustrate some of the tensions involved in conceptualising young people attending E2E programmes. As we saw in Chapter 4, Finlay *et al* (2010) caution against regarding NEET sub-groups as types with common needs, attitudes and responses. The fact that many young people share a particular characteristic does not mean this is their main distinguishing feature, or that other characteristics or aspects of their lives are at all similar to others in the same sub-group. A similar situation obtains in the case of programmes like E2E. Although specific needs or deficits may well be present in a number of learners, it is likely that their particular biographies and circumstances will underpin very different responses.

Furthermore, it is important to recognise the positive aspects which young people bring to such programmes, and our research evidence provides a rather different perspective on E2E learners than some of the discourse surrounding NEET young people might suggest. Half had experience of paid work, sometimes with self-employed parents or relatives. Although in general academic attainments were very modest, and the majority of GCSE grades obtained were in the range D-G, only a quarter of participants had no GCSE passes, and nearly half had one or more pass at grade C or above. A small number had relatively high attainment, with GCSE grades perfectly adequate for admission to A level programmes. Although aspirations for employment or further study tended to be limited, some participants aimed at university and professional occupations, and drew on family or friends for experience of work or higher education. It is enlightening to hear from Ruth again, later in her interview:

> With all this credit crunch it might sound stupid but you're always going to need teachers, aren't you? Well that's what I'm aiming for with Receptions and Year 1 because at the moment I'm a classroom assistant ... Voluntary on Fridays ... and then I will go on to do it as a placement. I like what I'm doing at school and realistically I am a teacher – because you are, aren't you? I'm doing everything that the teacher's doing. So I said that's really what I want to do and so [an E2E tutor] said that you don't necessarily have to go to university because I can do the Level 4 here.

High unemployment rates are common in the families of NEET young people, and in the UK as a whole, 26 per cent of 16-17 year olds who are NEET live in households without work (Barham *et al*, 2009:28). The young people in our research reflected this: ten out of 51 lived in households where no-one had paid employment at the time they were interviewed. However, these young people were by no means immersed in cultures of worklessness, and in most cases their families had some history of employment. This conflicted with perceptions within the partnership that intergenerational unemployment was a significant challenge in working with E2E learners:

> It's very hard to change the mindset of a young person who has come from three generations of unemployment, for example. But we do have a lot of providers who have got young people like that and I've always said that for one out of ten that you work with from that particular situation [E2E might be successful] – ten percent might seem very low but when you are looking at the fact that there isn't a work ethic there it's a major factor ... (E2E Partnership Manager)

Of the ten young people in non-working households, one lived with retired grandparents and one with a lone parent on maternity leave, two had parents recently made redundant and one had a lone parent prevented from working by caring responsibilities. In a global recession, the number of families without work was remarkably low. The family backgrounds of the E2E learners in our case-study sites were over-whelmingly those of people in relatively low-paid, unskilled or semi-skilled employment – what New Labour discourse referred to as 'hard-working families' and has now metamorphosed into the 'alarm-clock Britain' of the Coalition government. Parents' occupations included factory worker, supermarket assistant, cleaner, lorry driver, bottle packer, care assistant and sheet-metal worker (see Appendix 1). A small minority of parents in white-collar employment was represented, such as a primary schoolteacher and an accounts clerk, and several parents were self-employed. It may be, of course, that the young people in our case-study sites were untypical of the partnership as a whole; however, this seems unlikely and we suggest that the discourse surrounding NEET young people tends to highlight the situation of young people who conform to its stereotypes, constructing them as more typical than they really are.

Learning environments

Before analysing the educational processes taking place within E2E programmes, it is useful to consider the location of providers and the physical environments encountered within their premises. Studies of disadvantaged young people often emphasise the close ties they have with the neighbourhoods and other places they feel connected to and describe a marked reluctance to move away from safe territory for work, education or socialising (MacDonald *et al*, 2005). Although this is partly due to material factors such as travel costs and reliance on public trans-port, it can also derive from particular types of social capital acquired from family and friends living within the immediate neighbourhood. As Green and White (2008) suggest, such young people are often strong on *bonding* capital but less able to access *bridging* capital of the type that confers social advantage.

In our research, practitioners often referred to the reluctance of learners to travel between areas – for example, between the small towns in both authorities or across the larger towns. Learners themselves valued proxi-mity and this had often been a factor in deciding on a particular provider; some had withdrawn from other courses because of lengthy or difficult journeys. The E2E partnership, with its network of providers distributed across the two authorities, was well placed to attract young people for whom travel was difficult. To some extent, this helped maintain an ethos of care and nurture for learners, evident in all the provision we saw. In each provider, everyone knew everyone else and there was a strong integration of teaching, domestic and administrative functions. However, it also meant that learners and staff tended to be isolated from other areas of education and training, and limited the facilities available to both groups.

Within providers, the physical environment illustrates some of the material consequences of creating educational markets by drawing in private and voluntary sector organisations, particularly where lower-status provision is concerned. In view of the intention to use organisations with experience of working with disadvantaged young people, most E2E providers understandably concentrated on a limited number of courses and client groups, usually at the lower end of the academic and vocational scale. At Middlebridge College, although E2E was part of a large public-sector institution, the programme appeared quite separate from other courses, apart from some adjacent specialist provision for young people with learning difficulties. The E2E learners and staff were allocated to an older, less well-appointed part of the college, and learners accessed the building from a side street rather than the entrances used by the majority of college students. Craft workshops formerly used to teach joinery and metalwork had fallen into disuse, and one such area had recently been reclaimed by E2E:

> The workshop is a short walk from the office ... Gareth [E2E tutor] ... realised it wasn't being used so thought he'd put the resources to good use. This is a large space with thousands of pounds worth of equipment. Frank [part-time joinery teacher] explains that he used to use it to train young people for work but that the demand had since disappeared and so the space was left empty ... (Field notes, 27th November 2008 [quoted in Russell *et al*, 2011])

Workshop facilities were also available at providers with a craft orientation, and as we have seen, certain types of vocational learning encountered across the partnership – particularly hairdressing – were sometimes embedded in authentic working environments. In these providers, learning resources were limited, although basic skills materials and computer facilities were available within the spaces used by young people. In principle, learners could use the learning resource centre at Middlebridge College, but there was little evidence of this. In all the case-study sites, tutors arranged displays of work by current and previous learners, often illustrating aspects of the E2E programme, biographies of learners and the various progression routes available. As well as displays of work and educational posters, social control was evident through signs and notices which outlined penalties (including instant dismissal) for infringements of rules such as smoking and use of mobile phones.

In addition to the spatial separation between E2E provision and mainstream forms of post-16 learning, a temporal dislocation existed in which the roll-on, roll-off nature of E2E often conflicted with the conventional academic terms operated by other courses. Young people coming to the end of the programme could face a lengthy wait before progression opportunities became available, with a likelihood of becoming NEET in the meantime. Indeed, in 2009-10, the year following our research, around one-quarter of new entrants to the NEET category in Middlebridge consisted of E2E leavers (Russell *et al*, 2011). Even at the level of holidays, E2E learners receiving EMA experienced this temporal dislocation:

> Susanna talks about how they have to [manage] the Christmas break. Learners gather two days holiday per month worked on EMA, but many have not been here long enough to accrue such holidays to take over the Christmas period. Therefore they have had to give the learners a project to do over the two-week break. Susanna holds up her fingers to quote 'project' as she explains. They will break up on 19th December for two weeks. The college is shut over this period anyway. Susanna says, 'it's a joke'. (Field notes, 10th December 2008)

Learning activities

The experiences offered to learners in our case-study sites reflected the core curriculum of E2E discussed at the beginning of this chapter. Although the nature of the learning activities varied considerably, particularly as a result of the vocational orientation of the provider, all sites emphasised practical approaches to learning, often employing a discourse which described learners as averse to extended periods of classroom activity, particularly when writing was involved (see also James and Simmons, 2007). Enrichment activities were commonplace, and learners were taken on activities such as overnight stays in bunkhouses, hill walking and visits to places of interest. Formal teaching and learning tended to be associated with basic skills sessions, although tutors also embedded literacy and numeracy in practical tasks. The vocational orientation of a provider could be a useful focus for embedding these skills, and tutors working on the more general programme at Middlebridge College used an allotment to develop both literacy and numeracy.

The field note extracts below illustrate the learning experiences we encountered. The first, at Middlebridge College, shows young people designing greetings cards to be sold at the Christmas fair described in Chapter One. The extract begins at around 10.00am, following time set aside for the learners to socialise. The young people arrive from 9.00am onwards and relax for the next hour, chatting, playing computer games, listening to their iPods, and getting their own tea and biscuits. Various board games are available, and learners are encouraged to use them by the tutors. Today, the group of thirteen will be split into two, one group going to the workshop for joinery whilst the remaining learners work on the Christmas cards. In the afternoon, the groups will swap over.

10.00am Steve [tutor] asks who would like to go to the workshop for joinery, most say they'd prefer to stay here, but he manages to get a group together. The remaining learners sit down; Fran sits at the tutor's desk (although she often moves around the classroom during the session). She shows two cards she made earlier, the lads can't believe she made them herself. Fran asks how much they would pay for the cards. Some say £1, others 75p or £1.25. Fran explains that they need to make 50 cards to sell. Today they need to produce ideas, some of the learners move to the computers while others remain at their desks. Fran makes her way around the classroom, she asks, 'What's your idea, Adam?' He says, 'I don't know but I like to do my own ideas'. Fran says this is fine.

10.15am Fran asks what might go on a Christmas card. Some of the learners shout out ideas and Fran writes them down on the whiteboard: a Christmas tree, sleighs, Santa, reindeer ... Fran says, 'Well, it looks like we've got some good ideas.' Lewis is busy cutting out stencils, he asks, 'Does it 'ave to be perfect?' – Fran says no. Chris suggests, 'Why don't we sell them on this website?', he has found one that sells cards at £23 for ten. Fran asks, 'Well, how much is that each? Chris tries to work it out on a piece of paper

– Fran walks over to him and leans over the desks to see how he is working it out, she says, 'Do you want me to show you an easier way to do it?' and shows him the division.

10.20am Fran tries to motivate the learners by saying that the profit will go towards their day out. One lad asks, 'Is this a practice?' Fran says, 'Yes, why do you think we're doing that?' and he responds, 'So we don't fuck it up'. Fran says, 'So we don't mess it up, yeah.' Fran explains that the materials cost £40 so they need to be careful. The phone goes and Fran leaves the room to answer it. While she is absent, the class functions well. Two lads discuss the price of Christmas cards. One lad plays games on the computer. Ellie continues gluing. Another lad copies a picture of a bell. One lad uses the guillotine to cut some coloured paper. Chris and Adam are researching card designs using Google.

10.28am Fran returns and asks Leon to do some work (Leon has recently been involved in a serious car accident followed by plastic surgery. Fran later explains that he has been granted more time on E2E as he suffers with short-term memory loss, struggles to complete tasks and is much slower than some of the other learners). She says that they have had half-an-hour to do research and must now start work on their card designs. Fran helps Chris decide how to do his reindeer template. Chris says, 'I don't get it!' Fran explains that his reindeer image is quite complex and might be difficult, so she diverts his attention back to the whiteboard to see what might be an easier image ...

10.40am Fran sees what Jack is up to, she says he might want to use a different colour for his design, Jack jokes, 'That's racist!' Fran asks him what 'racist' means and he says he doesn't know. Chris asks why black people can call each other 'niggers' and white people can't and Fran explains that certain terms can be thought of as racist in different contexts. She explains that they should be mindful of other people's feelings. The discussion turns to 'Christmas' and should we continue to use that name. One lad asks why should people who enter England be offended by England's customs. Fran reminds them about the word 'goon', she asks do they remember its meanings (they have obviously had a conversation about this previously), one learner says it means a stupid person and Ellie says her mum calls her a goon. Fran says this might be interpreted as offensive language in the classroom.

...

11.40am The group start to tidy away for lunch. Jack clears his cuttings from the floor and Chris rolls his paper into a ball and launches it into the bin held high by Jack. Fran threatens them saying they must adhere to health and safety rules otherwise she will devote a whole day to reminding them what they are, Chris says, 'You can razzle!'

The second extract is from a vocational skills session at *Action for Youth*:

12.30pm The engineering department is a large, noisy work area inside the mill, with sections for welding, machinery and tools. Ian [vocational tutor] explains that the learners are working towards an NVQ Level 1. There are usually two members of staff here, but one is making a home visit. Ian explains that they are concerned about the personal hygiene of one lad and are thinking about buying him clothes at Matalan.

There are five white lads here. They come up to Ian to show him their welding: a corner piece of metal. Ian explains that they all make a tool box eventually, he shows me some examples. He would like a furnace so they could mould metal and do more things with the learners but is restricted due to insurance costs. Ian shows me some fencing that the lads are making for a butterfly quarter in a nearby park. They have to buy the moulded metal tops as they don't have a furnace but are constructing a see-through fence, so children can watch the butterflies.

One of the lads comes up to Ian to show him his work, Ian asks, 'Did you do the little C's?' as he moves his hands in a tiny C-movement indicating how they should weld. The lad admits that he didn't do this all the way. Ian says, 'Why not, you know it works!' The lad smiles, Ian says they can clean it up. The lad goes away to cool and clean his metal. Ian explains that they work better this way as it makes them nervous if he stands over them. He says that if an inspector was in he would watch over them and tick the worksheet boxes but [normally] finds the hands-off approach works best.

Ian explains that a lot of their learners are very good practically, but are not so academic, he says he explains to them they need both but empathises with their difficulties. He says one lad is ready for placement but there are none available. Ian explains that he is straight with the learners – he doesn't give them false hope, they are all too aware of the difficulties with obtaining placements. Some of the lads leave at 2.00pm. Ian explains that he lets them go once they have done their work. Officially he shouldn't, but doesn't understand the point of them staying when they have done their work. He says they could cause more danger by staying.

During the break Danny, a building maintenance tutor ... shows me a metal dragon made by learners, it is very impressive. He says the learners have sold such dragons on EBay. There is a wall that separates a classroom learning space from the messy work area full of paint, work benches and materials. This wall has cartoon images of young people dressed in [designer] gear. Danny explains that a learner did the artwork; he was poor in terms of literacy and numeracy but very skilful with a paintbrush. The learner was offered a job from one of his placements. He says there are some success stories, but like Ian explains the difficulty of finding placements. Many businesses have gone bust and [others] can't risk having a young person damage their reputation. (Field notes, *Action for Youth*, 29th January 2009)

These extracts illustrate the characteristics of teaching and learning in E2E programmes. A striking feature is the readiness of tutors to exploit the permeable boundaries between the three core curriculum areas in E2E, for example by taking opportunities to embed literacy and numeracy into vocational training sessions or to raise the awareness of learners by discussing general issues raised by instances of discriminatory language. Framing, or the amount of visible teacher control over pacing, selection of content and other aspects of the pedagogic environment (Bernstein, 1971) was relatively weak, with discourses of 'waiting for learners to come to you' and 'working at the learners' own pace' figuring prominently in tutors' explanations of pedagogy. Explicit pedagogy often dissolved into more generalised relationships between learners, tutors and other staff as the events of daily life – cooking meals, making tea for each other, listening to music – became part of the learning experience and provided a means to build confidence and trust. Informality was the norm, and most young people claimed to get on well with staff, frequently contrasting this with their experience at school. For many learners, being 'not like school' was a significant strength of the programme, and smaller groups, personal attention and being treated like adults were appreciated. Asked why she had returned to *MGC Training* after two other courses at the same provider had not worked out, Ruth replied:

> I liked it here. And it's not like at tech because tech is all, like, lectures but here you can sort of chill out and take your time and you don't have to get this done by so and so like you do at school. You can do it at your own pace … The staff you can get along with. They let you do as much as you can and they'll let you get away with so much, do you know what I mean? Swearing is one thing that they don't allow. I do like it here.

However, as Bernstein emphasised, framing is about visible rather than actual control, and regulation of time, behaviour, content and assessment was perhaps only superficially different from other spheres of education. Interestingly, there is some evidence amongst school-age learners that being treated in more adult ways in work-based learning environments can reinforce negative attitudes to school, and presumably to other formal learning settings (Hall and Raffo, 2004). Our research suggested that this may occur with E2E learners, as some contrasted its ethos with college courses as well as school; however, many still aspired to progress to such courses.

The focus on employability characteristic of E2E assumes the necessity of re-forming attitudes inimical to obtaining paid employment, and the work of tutors was largely concerned with developing attributes such as punctuality, a conventional personal appearance and interpersonal skills. Some providers replicated certain aspects of Fordist employment conditions, with clocking-in and buzzers for meal-times. Most tutors dressed according to workplace norms associated with the vocational focus of providers. In spite of a general informality, it was clear that one of the aims of E2E was to socialise learners into the norms and practices of work and learning.

Serious infringement of rules or persistent failure to meet targets could lead to exclusion from learning sessions and – in extreme cases – removal from the programme. Absence, even for one day, could mean forfeiting EMA for the week. Tutors identified unacceptable behaviour and discouraged the use of bad language or racist and sexist remarks. Punctuality at the beginning of sessions was encouraged, and routines such as cleaning and tidying-up after workshop or practical activities were more or less consistently enforced, usually in a low-key way without using formal sanctions. However, tutors were more relaxed as learning sessions progressed and it was not uncommon for learners to be allowed to leave early. This practice was often justified in terms of their being tired, having a short attention span or running health and safety risks if sessions were prolonged.

Tutors appeared to take for granted that a practical, hands-on approach was preferable. In general, the disrupted school careers, poor literacy skills and difficulties in maintaining concentration which affected many learners were taken to preclude more formal work based on school subjects or vocational knowledge of a theoretical nature. The response of young people to this discourse was complex (Thompson, 2011b). They appeared largely to accept that E2E was not about acquiring school-type knowledge, and to enjoy learning through practical activities. As one learner said during a literacy session, 'That's the point of being here, to not do exams'. However, although many learners had disliked school, this was often related to relationships with teachers, a feeling of anonymity in large and sometimes chaotic classes, and external life events. School knowledge as such was not universally rejected, and some learners expressed regret at not making the most of school. A few young people described themselves as academically able and, although learners only rarely contested the non-academic discourse, there were occasions when they asked for more challenging work in basic skills sessions.

These features of E2E raise questions about the increasing adoption of work-based learning as a panacea for disaffection. In England and else-where, young people who appear to reject schooling are constructed as unsuited to the normal curriculum and to require alternative provision – often located away from the school, or in specialist units within it – which draws on topics and activities assumed to motivate them. Such an approach removes these learners, not only from the school, but also from the mainstream. This may be justified if it can be shown that the attitudes and skills inculcated by work-based learning have significant labour market value or aid re-integration into high-status educational pathways. However, there is little evidence of this occurring, either in our research or elsewhere.

Hall and Raffo (2004) find that the benefits of work-based learning for 14 to 16 year olds do not readily transfer to school settings, partly because of academic resistance to vocational knowledge but also because of a disconnection between the forms of social and cultural capital required for success in either setting. In the USA, although noting a *prima facie* likelihood that vocational tracking would increase engagement with education, Kelly and Price (2009) found no substantial benefit of this nature. These findings are perhaps unsurprising when we recognise the complex, socially constructed nature of disaffection and disengagement. As Thomson and Russell (2009:429) observe, positioning certain young people as 'good with their hands, not with their heads' homogenises a disparate set of biographies, dispositions and abilities, and polarises the options available. Such discourses operate with an undifferentiated notion of constructs such as 'practical' and 'academic', placing basic skills and work-related learning in opposition to an academic curriculum and ultimately failing to confront wider issues concerning the relationship between young people, education and work.

Placements

Although placements had never been easy to find, economic recession had intensified the difficulty of providing learners with appropriate work experience. Practitioners identified a number of factors contributing to delays and problems in placing learners, with those in private sector providers more ready to focus on the shortcomings of young people rather than structural factors in the economy. However, most agreed that local employment conditions presented the greatest obstacle. A tutor at Middlebridge College reported contacting up to sixty employers without success. Similar experiences were reported elsewhere:

> I go out and plead ... I'll go and knock on the door and state my case. I mean my opening line is: 'It's not going to cost you anything' – which is what you've got to do because they are a business and some of the smaller ones can't afford anything. Just at the moment around here there is very little work available. My brother is doing engineering and I get a few from the trade because I know a lot of people but of all the companies I know around here there is only one that has got much of an order book really. All the rest are just ticking over so, obviously, they don't want a young lad in getting under their feet. (Placement officer, *Action for Youth*)

One young person at *Action for Youth* had recently returned from a work placement in the building trade, simply because the company concerned had 'run out of work'. This was particularly unfortunate as he reported having learned useful skills during his time at the company. Unusually, this young person had also been paid whilst undertaking his placement.

The personal qualities and biographies of young people were seen as having a significant influence. There was some suggestion that employers would prefer learners who showed obvious motivation:

> We get a wide range actually because usually after July they're the ones that really want to come to us ... and they're joining the week after they've finished school so they've got to be interested. And then we see what we have at the end of September with our other intake. But the ones from July are usually pretty good and they're the ones that get out on placements because they are usually keen and interested. And then every year will get some who have been sat at home for six months not doing anything and they take a lot more motivating and we have, like, attendance issues and things like that. (Placement officer, *Action for Youth*)

Nevertheless, some employers were helpful over placing young people with complex needs, and practitioners emphasised the importance of finding 'the right placement' for learners. The private-sector providers in particular claimed to have strong links with local employers, and had databases of companies they had worked with. The availability of placements varied with employment sector. For example, *MGC Training* found placements in social care relatively straightforward to find – often helped by the labour-intensive nature of this work – whereas the retail sector was considerably more problematic. In some cases, it appeared that unpaid labour from young people could be attractive to employers:

> If it's a new placement, we will approach [the employer] and tell them about what we do and ask whether they are prepared to take a young person. But before they do we will go out and do a health and safety check and make sure that everything is in order. And over time, when they've had one or two young people in there, they will offer it to someone else. And looking at it – not from a negative point of view but from a personal point of view of the company – it's a kind of free labour for them but also it helps the young person and a lot of the time they do get employment out of it. I mean we've had students go through different companies and been employed at the end of it – whether it's in a care home or retail. So there is that aspect too which is really rewarding. (Manager, *MGC Training*)

However, this attitude was rare, and employers were often reluctant to offer placements whilst making redundancies.

Many learners spoke of enjoying their placement and gaining useful skills, but others found placements less rewarding. Placements appeared to work best when carefully matched to the learner, and when they offered both challenge and the prospect of employment. Matt was placed with a web-design company and reported gaining new knowledge and practical skills 'on the computer side'; there was a possibility of employment, in-house training and day-release to college. Mary was placed with a telesales company, and identified with the company and the work she was doing. Like Matt, she appeared to have a prospect of employment. However, the work in some placements could be routine and was either unskilled or used skills already acquired by the learners, often through previous employment. Aisha described her placement at a clothing retailer as about doing very routine activities: 'Well, we have to unpack the stuff that comes in and things like that and just stand at the door and say hello to people coming in', whilst Kieran, placed at a charity shop, said that his main activities were helping with deliveries and sorting clothing.

Some learners reported feeling bitter when work experience did not lead to permanent employment. Although they began placements knowing these were only temporary, expectations sometimes increased as relationships developed with colleagues in the placement. Hannah, from *Aim for Work*, already had concurrent part-time employment at a high street store and, although she found the placement straightforward, was prepared to see it out provided it led to a job:

> I've been on a placement as well and basically they said there would be a job for me when I finished but that didn't happen so I quit because I want somewhere they will employ me ... If they were going to employ me they'd have probably been annoyed but if I knew that they were going to employ me then I would have stayed ... And it was a trek getting there really and it was a bit annoying doing that journey there and back and not getting nowt out of them. It was the fact that you're not getting anything out of it when you know they are using you. They were nice people and that ... I got a bit bored after a month but I thought I'd stay another month and they might employ me but they didn't. I mean I got on with them all but I feel a bit betrayed. (Hannah, *Aim for Work* [quoted in Russell *et al*, 2011])

Agency, culture and constraint

Youth transition research emphasising agency and choice must come to terms with the over-riding influence of social inequality, institutional forms and changing opportunity structures (Heinz, 2009). However, the role of individual agency cannot be neglected, and was evident within our case-study sites. All providers stressed the need for learners to develop independence; both tutors and learners talked about an adult environment. The pedagogies articulated by tutors emphasised that young people learn better when self-motivated and can learn at their own pace, matching learning to their individual needs. To some extent, the differing specialisations of providers allowed learners to opt for programmes suited to their interests and vocational aspirations, although sometimes they had to accept places wherever available. Nearly all learners aspired to specific occupational or educational progression, and could identify pathways to help them achieve this. However, learner agency was constrained by broad cultural and structural factors. This section discusses the evidence relating to these factors, including the gendering of provision, constraints arising from ethnicity and religion, and the effects of learner expectations and parental attitudes.

Gender

Work-based learning tends to be populated largely by males, and low-attaining young women are more likely to participate in full-time education than young men with similar educational backgrounds. Gender differences have decreased slightly since the 1990s, but girls are still less likely to enter work-based pathways such as apprenticeships: for 16 to 18 year olds in 2009, 5.2 per cent of girls compared with 7.5 per cent of boys were in work-based learning (DfE, 2010a). During the period of our research, around 60 per cent of E2E learners nationally were male. Although the overall gender distribution of the learners we interviewed reflected this, the proportions varied between providers, largely corresponding to their vocational focus (see Table 1.2). Although there was no evidence that providers actively recruited learners along gendered lines, enrolments reflected traditional gender roles, with boys making up the great majority of learners at *Action for Youth* and Middlebridge College, whilst the proportions were reversed at the other two providers, which focused on office administration, retail and social care. In providers specialising in traditionally male employment, girls often did not stay long, leaving for college courses or other providers. Those who remained were not necessarily committed to the provider's specialism; for example, one female learner who had enjoyed taking part in joinery sessions wanted a job in animal management.

In some cases, this gender imbalance led to the isolation of learners, and we noted one young woman in particular – the only female in a group of males at *Action for Youth* – who worked separately in preparation for an online basic skills test later that day. Asked about this, she replied, 'There is another lass here but she's not here today. It's alright. I talk to some of the lads but some of them I don't like because they're cocky'. Diana had arrived from another provider, where learners 'were mainly lasses', having been one of several young people who 'walked out' because their EMA was stopped due to lateness. Diana's options were limited because her youth offending prevented her from pursuing childcare, her original preference. She had begun to learn motor vehicle maintenance, but disliked it and, although she intended to remain at this provider, she aimed to acquire the qualifications needed to realise her new aim of office work. There was no evidence that joining the predominantly male environment at *Action for Youth* was an attempt to enter traditionally male employment; rather, it appeared to be the result of a progressive narrowing of Diana's options due to contingent events.

Ethnicity

Young people from ethnic minority groups are relatively poorly represented in work-based learning. Although average levels of educational achievement amongst young people of Pakistani, Bangladeshi and Black Caribbean descent are lower than for young white people (DCSF/ONS, 2009), they are more likely to participate in full-time post-compulsory education. Higher participation rates are particularly marked for those with low attainment at age 16 (Payne, 2003:38-39). By contrast, young people from ethnic minority groups are less likely to choose work-based learning (DCSF/ONS, 2009), and negative perceptions of work-based learning, particularly where lower-status routes are involved, have been reported amongst young people from Asian and Black Caribbean backgrounds (Foskett and Hemsley-Brown, 2001). These trends help to explain the relatively low proportion of learners from ethnic minority groups in our case-study sites which, although representative of the local population, is much lower than the proportions in local schools (31% in Middlebridge and 17% in Greenford). In addition to the low overall numbers of learners from ethnic minority backgrounds, it needs to be borne in mind that only a narrow range of ethnicities were represented amongst the learners we interviewed. They were a small minority of our sample, and all were from Pakistani, Bangladeshi or Black Caribbean/White mixed heritage backgrounds.

Our data suggested that gender and ethnicity interact in complex ways. Although our interview sample contained few young women from Pakistani or Bangladeshi backgrounds, in certain areas – particularly in parts of Greenford – the proportion of girls from Asian backgrounds was much higher than elsewhere in the partnership. This appeared to reflect, not only the make-up of local communities, but also the vocational focus and gender balance of providers. Parents of Asian-heritage learners, and the young people themselves, seemed much more comfortable with their daughters attending certain providers. These tensions could limit access to E2E:

> [A Connexions PA] explains the importance of ethnicity in terms of access. He talks about one Asian-origin female who was stopped from coming to the provider as she needed access to a mobile phone and her parents did not want this. He says there is a real issue about Asian females' parents worrying about them mixing too intently with white lads. (Field notes 8 January 2009 [quoted in Russell *et al*, 2011])

For learners of both sexes, their family and cultural ties with the Indian subcontinent could conflict with progression from school. In one case, Issaq had missed out on enrolment because he was visiting family in September: 'I was in Pakistan and I wanted to do an apprenticeship in electrical but I came back too late to apply for it'. A missed college enrolment day was also reported by Mehrun, a young woman taking childcare at *MGC Training*, and Aamerah at *Aim for Work* had started sixthform a month late, leaving after one term, although bulimia may have been the major issue, rather than the late start.

Some caution is needed in interpreting such accounts, for it is easy to make unfounded generalisations about Asian Muslim culture as inevitably constraining and part of the barriers to learning that young people on E2E programmes face. Shain (2003), for example, challenges conceptions of an isolated culture which hampers the development of girls in particular. She argues that, rather than being passive victims of oppressive cultures, Asian girls actively engage in producing identities drawing on both a residual home culture and the local cultures of the regions where they live. As with young white people, emerging identities are the outcome of many factors and not just the deterministic transmission of monolithic and limiting perspectives.

For the relatively small number of Asian-heritage E2E learners interviewed, aspirations appeared to be high. There was evidence of strong parental support, and high expectations. The following extract from Aisha's interview illustrates several of the issues discussed above:

> I'm doing work experience in [a women's clothing retailer]. Sometimes 9 to 5 and sometimes if they've got a lot of staff then they say 10 till 2. It's alright but sometimes it gets a bit tiring because you're just standing on your feet all day. I'm on placement Monday, Tuesday and then Thursday and Friday and I come here [to do maths and English] on Wednesday afternoons.

> My dad is working and he travels to London. He works at [a security firm]. And my mum stays at home. My brother is older [than me] and my sister is younger. She's still at school and my brother's at university.

> I went to college and did IT but I didn't want to carry on doing it so I [left] ... and then came here. The course was good but I just had to come out ... it was too far. The college was really far from the house. [My parents] didn't really mind because they knew that I didn't really like it and this is closer. I was planning to go to university but I need to get my maths and English because you need those to get in ... I want to get at least Cs ... and I'm doing an NVQ in customer service. [My parents] want me to get a degree or something because they expect a lot from me. [In between] I might go to another college and do another year of maths and English and try to do better so that I can get into [the local] university because I'm not sure my English is good enough so I just want to get that better. I can't start until September so I hope to stay here because they said I could stay here to get my customer service.

Learner orientations and parental attitudes

In Paul Willis's classic ethnography of resistance and social reproduction, the oppositional behaviour of a group of working-class 'lads' (Willis, 1977) expresses an ideology grounded in the masculine shopfloor cultures of family members and older peers from similar backgrounds. Willis found this ideology to be ultimately self-defeating, because the practices of resistance in which the lads engage tend to distance them from the social and cultural capital necessary for success in the dominant society. As we have seen, since the late 1970s globalisation and the increasingly competitive individualism of education and working life have further eroded the capacity for collective action. Consequently, resistance becomes marginalised as deviant behaviour, easy to position as disruptive and inferior. Perhaps even more so than in the 1970s, working-class kids who embrace such oppositional behaviour continue to get working-class jobs, if they get jobs at all. Willis's work has been criticised for its excessive focus on a particular sub-group of working-class young people which, some argue, is not typical of the group as a whole. However, whilst he does neglect young female cultures of resistance and submission, Willis does recognise a spectrum of responses found in different groups of working-class boys.

Brown (1987) proposes a more complex understanding of orientations towards schooling, in which many young people accept that compliance with the school ethos and the pursuit of academic qualifications are necessary for decent jobs. Those who are entirely alienated, or see academic knowledge as intrinsically worthwhile, are comparatively rare in most schools. According to Brown, the great majority of young people – the ordinary kids – have instrumental orientations, and it would be a mistake to conflate working-class cultures with a rejection of education. For a young person, there are different ways of being working-class or middle-class, which depend on the material and cultural resources available to them.

The variety of orientations outlined above was reflected in our research. At one extreme, some young people appeared to parallel aspects of Willis's lads, displaying signs of alienation at an earlier age. Tom, a 17-year-old whose mother and father worked in a bank and as a self-employed sheet-metal worker respectively, was actively looking for work – although he 'didn't know' what kind of work he preferred – and hoped to leave soon for a job in a factory. His parents liked him being on a course, but wanted him to find work. Tom thought that E2E was 'alright' but disliked basic skills. He received EMA but claimed to 'spend it on drink':

> I did some voluntary work at _____ Park. Like helping out. I did, like, a two year work experience when I were at school for one day a week and it were with, like, a gardener in Rochdale .... I got thrown out of school in Year 7 [for] swearing at the teacher and I threw the chair at him. I didn't want to go back. I didn't like it at all ... and in Year 8 I had a year off school. Just staying at home. Then I went to a school in Rochdale [which closed] and then to

> _____. [After I left school] I got a part time job over here and then a proper job as a kitchen porter ... [I didn't like school] because I used to do nowt.
>
> [E2E is alright], it keeps me out of trouble and out of bed. I just want to come here and get me own money. I'm waiting for a job and when I get a job I'll leave here. Someone is meant to be ringing me about this job because my auntie works there and she's trying to get me a job and that because they are taking people on and she is meant to be ringing me about it. (Tom, *Action for Youth*)

Orientations towards participation could change over time, although one should be cautious about inferring more profound transformations than might be explained by the adoption of a more instrumental stand-point. Mary, an 18-year-old learner at *Aim for Work*, was 'bored all the way through high school' and had 'no idea' what GCSE grades she had achieved, although she knew that she had passes in English, RE, science, IT and childcare. Going home was the thing she liked best about school. After GCSEs, Mary started a childcare course at college, which was interrupted by illness; she then moved to *MGC Training* to continue with childcare, but was 'kicked out' following 'too many warnings for being disruptive'. After this, she worked part-time as a cleaner but eventually returned to education, taking business administration in an E2E programme:

> It was my second back-up plan if I didn't like child care. It was something I enjoyed doing. Me and my friend wanted to come here because we got fed up being cleaners and I just asked my Connexions advisor if he could get me in ... [I didn't want to do childcare anymore as] I'm fed up of looking after both my parents at home. [When I was doing childcare] they weren't that ill ... so I didn't look after them that much and I just loved working with kids but then I got fed up of looking after everybody at once. My mum's got a bad back and arthritis so she can't walk far and my dad's got loads of stuff wrong with him but it's too much to talk about. [They need me to do the] cleaning and cooking – that's the main thing, they can do some stuff themselves but they find it hard to do it all. I do have help from my neighbours and they are really good. [My parents] want me to do really well and they did actually have an input on me coming back into college because I wasn't going to come back to college; I was going to carry on being a cleaner and try and get another job but they kind of persuaded me to come back.

Although Mary had been alienated from school, her attitude appeared to have changed :

> I haven't a bad word to say about E2E. It's relaxed. If you're doing maths and English and stuff you just go at your own pace and they help you whereas at high school there would be, like, 30 other people and the teachers wouldn't have the time to help me but here they do find the time to help.

A number of young people used a discourse of progression towards personal goals to express more positive orientations towards learning. However, they recognised the reality of adverse labour markets and the difficulty of overcoming early educational disadvantage. Many learners just wanted a job, and were happy to consider similar occupations to their parents, although it was common for parents to want their children to do better than they had.

Where possibly unrealistic aspirations existed, there could be difficulties in providing careers advice which reconciled personal ambition with reality. In the case of Shannon, who talked of eventually becoming a dentist, it seemed that practitioners were more comfortable with the well-trodden paths of other learners in similar circumstances than with helping her to find pathways related to her dreams. Shannon lived independently and had little contact with her parents; she had been 'kicked out' of home in Year 11 due to a difficult relationship with her mother. She ceased attending school for a while, although she returned to take her GCSEs, achieving grade D in maths, science and English – having been predicted to achieve B grades before leaving home:

> I came to college in September and I was on Business Admin [Level 2] but I quit because it was too boring. I just told [my Connexions PA] that it was too boring and I decided to quit. I actually do want to go back on that course but at the time I was just moving on and it were just too boring. I couldn't cope. And I didn't like the people on the course neither.

> Every time you go to Connexions they don't really help me. If I went in and I said that I wanted to be a dentist I would just get sent from person to person and no one really knows. When I signed up for business I didn't really know what I wanted to do so the woman signed me up for business. There is no bad thing [about E2E] but if I could do anything [else] I wouldn't choose to be here. I'd rather do a course in September. I'm just here to pass time, to be honest. It is a good course and that and it does help you because you do key skills and that gets you up to a grade C in maths and English. But I'd rather do something a bit more ... [focused]. Because say if I'd just stuck to business I wouldn't be here. I would never have chosen this course as like, this is what

I want to do. I just chose it because I had nothing else to do. And because it was half way through the year and all the other college courses had started I decided to come here. Yeah. I'm going enrol again in September. I know I want to be a dentist [although] I only want to be a dentist because they make lots of money.

The situation regarding E2E learners, their educational and family backgrounds, and the exercise of individual agency is far more complex than presented in some of the policy discourse on NEET young people. Our research found little evidence that cultures of worklessness and benefit dependency are becoming ingrained, or that families and communities transmit antisocial attitudes or an antipathy to education. As Russell *et al* (2011) point out, although educational and social disadvantage affect many young people attending E2E programmes, they do not appear to be fundamentally different to working-class learners in general. Although many E2E learners show signs of disaffection or disengagement, these are better understood through the specific circumstances and biographies of young people in relation to the broader contexts of education, work and society. As we have seen in Chapter 4, concepts such as disaffection and disengagement are often used in a normative way, presenting disconnection from privileged forms of activity as a function of individual deficits. The evidence from our research is that considerably more sophisticated approaches to understanding these issues are required.

Just as the orientations of learners towards participation were complex and multi-faceted, the influence of parents appeared to vary a great deal. Some resisted participation in E2E. Although in some cases this appeared partly due to a wish for their children to gain employment as soon as possible, more complex reasons could underlie such opposition. Negative perceptions of E2E were not uncommon, and practitioners spoke of schools, parents and young people seeing the programme as remedial provision for failing or disruptive pupils. However, this perception was changing with greater contact between providers and schools, as well as through the agency of learners.

[My mum] didn't like the idea of me coming ... on E2E because you know what mums are like ... they all talk about this stuff and she got the wrong idea from people ... she thought it was, like, where all the troubled teens go and all, like, people who got kicked out of school and that. But I've explained to her that it isn't. [And my] friend came here and she explained to my mum that it's not like that. (Donna, *MGC Training*, 30 March 2009)

For another parent, opposition was based on the concern that more education would simply mean more failure; again, this view changed with time:

> When I left school and was still living at home they said to me: try your best to get a job because college is the last resort. I wanted to go to college at first but I didn't get in. My mum and dad really didn't want me to go because they wanted me to earn money. They'd seen that I'd messed up in school so they didn't want me to go to college and mess that up also. But now I'm on this course and they can see that I'm changing and they know that this time I'm not going to let them down. (Ruth, *MGC Training* [quoted in Russell *et al*, 2011])

Although most young people appeared to value parental approval, this was not always forthcoming, even after some time. But they still gained a sense of achievement from learning new skills and finding opportunities for progression:

> She were expecting me to come out of school with – well I did come out with nowt but she just expects me to do shit and that but I've got a place in college now. I applied a bit ago and I've just got in now. ... Some of the stuff I've learnt in the workshop and that, with making things ... people I know have already said to me 'Make me this and I'll pay you'. If people start doing that you can make your own business ... I've made a couple of things for people. (Phil, *Action for Youth* [quoted in Russell *et al*, 2011])

The struggle and contestation between young people and their parents over post-16 decisions was not always resolved. Some learners simply went their own way, relying on personal feelings and the advice of friends and practitioners to validate their choices. The non-academic nature of E2E could intensify these struggles. For Hannah, school had not been enjoyable and she truanted 'quite a bit' in Years 10 and 11. Nevertheless, she achieved good GCSEs in eight subjects and began A-levels in Psychology, Travel and Tourism and Photography at her school sixth-form. However, she found the transition from GCSE difficult, and left in January.

> [My dad] weren't happy. My mum is just one of those people who will just go with it and if she knows you don't like it she thinks 'Well, I can't force her to

do it' but my dad doesn't like that and he says: 'You're ruining your life; you're going to end up like your mum'.

She's just a cleaner but, like, she hasn't really done what she'd like. She's alright about it and she has got a job and stuff. She's an alright mum and stuff but my dad can't say much really because his relationships have always been bad and I've had a few problems with them as well and that's upset me ... I'm one of them people, like, if I'm going to do something I'll do it but my dad just said that if I didn't stay at sixth form I'd end up here with rubbish grades. (Hannah, *Aim for Work*)

Heinz (2009) emphasises the role of resources in young people's school-to-work transitions, arguing that differential access to material and cultural capital will mediate their ability to co-ordinate biographical timings with those that are institutionally and culturally defined, particularly in the face of personal crises and other events. Put bluntly, the less money one has, the more difficult it is to adhere to the agendas of post-16 education and employment markets. As Heinz points out, young people with few opportunities or resources have little chance to assess circumstances and construct a desired future. They may opt for less satisfactory pathways as they present themselves, minimising immediate risk but sacrificing long-term gains. Hannah describes the impact of her need to earn money:

I'm getting to that point now where I've had work experience in an office and if it comes to it when I apply for an office job I can say that I've had that experience. So now I'm just looking for any job because I owe my dad two hundred quid so I want any job that will get me some money. I do want to do full time though because if I get full time I can have my weekend off ... [I'm not going on to college], I can remember when I left sixth-form I said [to my friends] that I'm leaving now and I know that by the end of the year I bet half of you will leave as well ... And about five of them left and I knew they would. So they spent all that time there and still didn't get any qualifications.

To be honest, if I get a full time job I'm off. I need money ... I sent off for this accountancy thing and it were like an apprenticeship because you get a placement but, at the same time, you get a proper wage because it's like working for a proper company. I'd like to do accountancy while I'm here but if I get a full-time job I'm just going to leave because I've had that experience in an office and I'm glad about that. I'd prefer to get a job in admin or if I could get one in accountancy and that one I were saying about was, like, a proper wage but you were getting training at the same time.

In spite of impatience amongst many learners to move on or find employment, most of the young people interviewed spoke highly of E2E and felt that the programme was helping them to achieve longer-term goals. Other research indicates that young people remain optimistic about the future and feel that vocational education can provide an alternative route to success (Bathmaker, 2005:86), although not all studies support this (Rudd and Evans, 1998). At the same time, E2E learners were acutely aware of their positioning in the educational hierarchy and did not expect to find employment easily. Perhaps more than anyone, the young people themselves appreciated the limits of their agency.

6

The Tutors' Story: Professional practice and pedagogy in E2E

This chapter explores the working lives of the adults – particularly tutors and Connexions workers – who are responsible for the learning of young people attending E2E and similar programmes. We draw on our ethnographic data to examine the biographies of these practitioners, the ways in which they relate to the young people under their guidance, and the relationship between the discourses they employ and the pedagogies they adopt. The chapter begins by discussing the context of teaching in the FE system as a whole, and the debates around professionalism that have dominated teacher development in the sector over the last twenty years. Taking up some of these wider themes, we examine how tutors become involved with E2E, the professional identities they acquire and the approaches to workforce development which underpin the experiences of individual tutors.

Explaining the conceptual framework of a major research project into learning and teaching in further education, James and Biesta (2007) emphasise the social nature of learning, as something that is not merely 'done' but 'done with others' (p23). They regard the expressions, dispositions and practices of learners and tutors as constructing the learning culture of an educational institution, and place their research findings within this context. Drawing on their work, we develop an account of learning cultures in our case-study sites, focusing particularly on the discourses tutors use to describe learners and frame pedagogy. To understand the work of these tutors, it is important to look at the discursive frameworks in which they operate – particularly those relating to NEET young people. Discourses involve much more than a particular use of language; they are 'practices that systematically form the objects of which they speak' (Foucault, 1989:54). They regulate what can be discussed in a particular context. And they govern who is entitled to speak and what they can say, thereby structuring our perceptions and limiting how we conceive the possibilities of action. The interactions of biography, discourse and pedagogy are a central part of how we understand the work of E2E tutors.

Teachers and tutors in further education

The English FE system was for many years something of a backwater, attracting little attention from non-specialists and largely outside public and political consciousness, which traditionally focused on higher-profile issues such as transformations within the school system and the expansion of higher education. Nevertheless, large numbers of people experienced further education, often through day-release or evening attendance at vocational training courses, or by taking part in adult education classes. The long-standing emphasis in FE on vocational training for employed young people and adults was disrupted by economic and social factors from the mid-1970s onwards, with the result that for large numbers of students FE colleges were now a continuation of school and a substitute for work, rather than a part of vocational development and progression.

Teaching in further education has traditionally been characterised by tensions and contradictions. On the one hand, class-based attitudes to vocational education have depressed the status of vocational teachers, who tended to be overlooked in the restructuring of school teaching by the Conservative governments of the 1980s. In spite of an increasing policy focus on the economic role of further education, FE teachers continued to be largely neglected. Pay and conditions, once relatively generous in order to attract teachers from industry, deteriorated significantly in comparison with those for schoolteachers. In spite of repeated attempts to raise the status of FE teaching and introduce some form of compulsory training, it was not until the advent of New Labour – with its slogan 'Education, education, education' – that this was achieved. However, as Thompson and Robinson (2008) argue, the reforms introduced between 2001 and 2007 were in many ways a missed opportunity, and in spite of rhetoric about professionalisation, they left unchallenged the differential status of vocational teaching and the weak regulation of entry to this occupation.

Although many FE teachers are graduates, their qualifications are often below degree level, and many have limited experience of academic study. New teachers are largely recruited directly from industry, and the overwhelming majority follow an in-service training route rather than acquiring a teaching qualification prior to employment. Until 2001, there was no official requirement to obtain a recognised teaching qualification even following employment, although many providers had policies which encouraged their staff to become teacher-trained. A plethora of qualifications existed, including both university awards and qualifications offered by national awarding bodies – some of which were highly specific, competence-based, and geared towards limited occupational roles such as assessor. From 2001 onwards, legislation required newly-employed teachers who were not already trained to obtain an approved teaching qualification. However, this measure was only partially successful, and government impatience with the rate of progress towards a professionalised workforce led to further reforms. A new professional body was introduced, alongside a national qualifications structure comprising a system of awards which in some ways was divisive and open to abuse.

Whilst the reforms introduced a more demanding qualification for staff in a full teaching role, they also institutionalised lesser qualifications for an associate role which is increasing in prominence as providers work with more diverse student bodies and imperatives towards personalised learning create more demand for learning support. The associate teacher role enables the employment of less well-qualified staff in these support functions, usually on less favourable conditions. Furthermore, newly appointed teachers in either a full or associate teaching role have up to five years to complete the relevant qualification – which can mean, in a sector where high staff turnover is not uncommon, that teachers may complete lengthy periods of service with one or more providers without ever becoming fully trained. As a result, progress towards professionalisation has been slow (Thompson, 2010).

The notion of teacher professionalism in FE is contested, and has been approached in various ways since the mid-1990s, when processes of marketisation and managerial control led to the virtual reconstruction of the sector (Shain and Gleeson, 1999). Robson (2006) argues that professionalism represents a set of cultural and social practices for organising the work of individuals and institutions, proposing that traditional characteristics of a profession, such as autonomy, specialist knowledge and a service ethos, are still relevant, in spite of the effects of managerialism and performativity. However, professionalism has always led a precarious existence in FE and cannot be presented as part of a lost golden age; it must be understood as a contextually sensitive concept, constructed through the practices and discourse of teachers, managers and officials.

For some authors, conflict and change over the last twenty years have proletarianised FE teaching, with teachers in the sector deskilled and closely surveilled along the lines of Fordist employment. Others take a more nuanced approach, emphasising the complexity of FE and recognising deficiencies in the way the sector was run prior to incorporation (Avis, 2007). From this point of view, these years have seen processes of de-skilling, re-skilling and upskilling operating simultaneously. Such contradictory currents have opened up possibilities for FE teachers to create identities which combine residual elements of a public service ethos with new constructions of what it means to be a good FE teacher – including flexibility, entrepreneurship and an emphasis on student welfare.

It is against this backdrop that we must examine the work of E2E tutors. Recruitment, training and development, professional identities, and the pedagogies which tutors draw upon, must all be placed within the context of FE professionalism in general, whilst recognising the particular conditions of E2E. In some respects, the distinctive features of FE practice are sharpened and intensified in work-based learning, where cultural histories can be shorter and more vulnerable than elsewhere in FE, and tutors' identities must contend with prevailing discourses of NEET young people. Although a growing body of research has examined FE professionalism, and the importance of biography and its interactions with the context and culture of the workplace is increasingly recognised (Hodkinson and Hodkinson, 2004; Jephcote and Salisbury, 2009), the great majority of this research has been concerned with teachers in FE colleges, and the work of E2E tutors has until now remained largely unexplored.

Biographies of tutors – becoming an E2E practitioner

It is comparatively rare for FE teaching to be a first career choice. The nature of further education is such that people tend to come from vocational backgrounds associated with their teaching subjects, or to have transferred to FE from schoolteaching. The circumstances surrounding entry to a first teaching post are therefore diverse, and it is not unusual for people to obtain employment with little or no formal training or background in teaching (Gleeson and James, 2007). The weak regulation of entry to FE teaching means that accidental or opportunistic contact with teaching and a largely unplanned growth of involvement – what Gleeson *et al* (2005) describe as 'sliding' into the job – are frequently evident. Furthermore, modernising approaches to FE management have reinforced rather than challenged flexible and casualised employment practices in the sector.

These general features were evident in the case of E2E tutors and other staff in our case-study sites, particularly those working for private and voluntary providers. For example, Tara, an E2E trainer at *Aim for Work*, illustrates the often opportunistic beginnings of work with young people and the function of part-time work as a 'long interview' (Gleeson *et al*, 2005:450) which could lead to full-time employment:

> When I moved to Middlebridge I was job hunting and I wasn't successful at all being in a new area and stuff so I was signing on for a little while [and looking for] business admin related work. I did bits here and there but nothing that would be a long-term career. I ended up in the New Deal [and] when I was working on my CV, I was approached by a tutor who said there was a job going at Connexions so I applied for it and got in. I was there for about two and a half years and then I applied for *Aim for Work* and I've been here since ... I came on the admin side and I was the receptionist here and within six months I had the opportunity to work on the E2E programme which I applied for and got the job.

Other tutors also described how finding administrative work in training providers, or attending courses in these organisations, could lead to teaching appointments or other work with young people; returning to work after raising a family, redundancy and relocation were all cited as factors in becoming an E2E practitioner. Gleeson *et al* (2005:450) quote one of their respondents as remarking '... nobody leaves school saying, Oooh, I want to be a basic skills teacher! It's something you come to by a variety of routes'. For many of our participants, the idea of teaching had come relatively late in life. However, experience of working with young people in other ways, and aspirations to do more, had often existed for some time:

> I've worked in education for twelve years. I started as a helper [in schools] when my children were young ... Then I went to college for a learning support course [and] started being a classroom assistant and helping out there. I was a school governor for eight years doing special needs and I worked basically in groups in classrooms and I've worked from Reception right up to Year 6 and I also worked in primary and nursery because they set up a nursery at the school. So I've worked right across the ages from three to nineteen. And then I ended up teaching a little bit as well and I taught art to Years 5 and 6. I did after school clubs and also residential trips and stuff.
>
> Eventually I thought I wanted a change because when I had my children I was working part time and, unfortunately, there were no full time jobs in the school so I thought that I needed a change in my career. I still liked the education side so I applied for a job at *MGC Training* and I started there as a tutor [with] 16 to 19 year olds. I enjoyed that and then a line manager in my department went on maternity leave ... she had twins and preferred to stay at home to look after them so I ended up with the role of cross-centre manager. So I came fairly new to Greenford but I knew the place and I knew the staff fairly well so I've been pretty happy there. (Jenny, Manager at *MGC Training*)

Other participants also spoke of long-term interests in education and ambitions to work with young people. Susanna, an E2E key worker at Middlebridge College, had 'always wanted to be a teacher of some description or to work in helping people'; Ian had worked in engineering for over ten years but decided on a career change at the age of forty, having 'always had an interest in teaching', and became a tutor at *Action for Youth*.

The diversity of backgrounds and routes into teaching which characterise FE tutors in general is discussed by Jephcote *et al* (2008), who remark on the influence of their often chequered educational histories and the ways in which they draw on their later development to inform their work with learners, seeing themselves as role models for a future generation of young people who make good through further education. This was the case with many E2E tutors:

> My secondary education was, can we say, interrupted! I was born and raised [here] and ... I passed the 11+ exam and went to technical school but my father moved, with his job, to Darlington [where] there was just a grammar or a secondary modern. I did the entrance test but didn't get enough for the grammar school so they put me in the secondary modern. I did three years there and then came back [here] for the last year ... they put me in a secondary modern and everything was different: they were doing German whereas I'd been doing French; I'd been in basic science classes whereas they were doing physics, chemistry – I was just totally lost and not a hope of catching up so when I was fifteen I thought I'd get myself a job. So I went out and got an apprenticeship. (John, *Action for Youth* [quoted in Thompson (2010)])

Many of the practitioners in our case-study sites had clearly embraced the possibilities of lifelong learning, from which employment contacts as well as qualifications could flow:

> Well I do have a Level 3 Child Care diploma which actually was when I was running a play group. So I've got all that as well ... I was doing a Level 2 literacy course and a Level 1 in my maths but when I started a couple of sessions up at college on my maths the tutor said that I was a Level 2 but when I got my job I couldn't continue the maths but I did a Level 2 here. And I'm doing a Customer Service Level 3 and that's ongoing.

> I started here through another member of staff who said there was a job going for a placement officer. She rang me up when I was at college doing [the] literacy course and said did I have my CV on me and could I come down and see K_____ who, at the time, was managing E2E. So I came down and had a look round and I thought it was brilliant, then I went for an interview and I got the job. But when I actually started they said that I'd got more qualifications and I could be a tutor, so I became a tutor for three days and then they asked me to go full time. (Liz, *MGC Training*)

Thompson (2011b) suggests that tutors draw on such life histories as a form of symbolic capital, establishing an authority over young people by means of credentials such as similar school experiences to learners, a background in employment sectors with which they can identify, and even vocationally-specific modes of dress. One tutor had attended a

YTS scheme after leaving school; another spoke of experiencing a rough approach to discipline as a young worker from a boss who later became his mentor and friend. In general, tutors positioned themselves as down-to-earth, with an understanding of the lives of learners and unlike the teachers whose attitudes young people frequently cited as contributing to alienation from school. At the same time, these tutors had ultimately adapted to education rather than rejecting it, demonstrating to learners that pragmatic compliance rather than resistance is the way to get on in life. Within such practices, biography is transformed into something like a negotiable capital, a means of exchange and accommodation with the cultural capital held by learners. Although this might provide an initial legitimacy for tutors working with young people in challenging circumstances, it does not necessarily lead to deeper forms of learning (Gleeson *et al*, 2005:453).

As we saw in Chapter 5, E2E providers were expected to offer specialist expertise, and some practitioners had a considerable depth of experience gained from their work on earlier programmes for marginalised young people and adults. Those who had been with E2E providers for a number of years had often seen several of these programmes:

> I worked on a few programmes before I came to this. I've worked here for nine years. When I first came here it were the adult programme which used to be called Pre-Vocational ... and it were for people from the age of 25 or so to 60 and that was quite interesting because a lot of them were sent from the Job Centre and didn't really want to be here. Then after that I went to work on a Life Skills programme which was funded through the DSS and it were basically getting them just to come in. People who are now, like, in NEET. It's that first port of call, isn't it? And I worked with them for quite a few years. Then I started doing youth training after that and then E2E. So I've had a bit of experience with both adults and younger people with similar issues ... (Sarah, *MGC Training*)

> I've always wanted to be a teacher of some description or to work in helping people – and maybe that's where I found E2E as a balance because you are a teacher but also you are offering that support and I like that balance ... I worked here [in the college] when the apprenticeship was starting in 2002 and I ended up helping out ... I was in a research role, researching why people were dropping out of the apprenticeships and I did that straight after uni [where] I did sociology. So I started here for a year but, at the same time, I was helping out on what was Life Skills at the time and E2E is based on the

Life Skills model ... So that's the background and that's how I started it but I knew I wanted to do something along those lines ... (Susanna, Middlebridge College)

Very few practitioners regretted coming into E2E teaching. The great majority found their work satisfying and some contrasted it strongly with previous employment, not only because it enabled them to play a worthwhile part in the lives of young people, but also because they enjoyed the nature of the teaching involved. The work could be stressful, and many of the tutors found learners frustrating at times, but for most these difficulties were offset by the rewards – particularly the opportunity to see young people responding, developing and building strong relationships with staff. Occasionally, former learners would return to talk about what they were doing. Gillian, a manager at *Action for Youth*, summed up the contrasts involved: 'I enjoy it. Every day is different. Sometimes it can be harrowing; sometimes it can be funny; sometimes I tear my hair out. But there is something different every day'. The staff at *Action for Youth* often took young people hill-walking, and this type of activity was greatly valued: 'Coming from manufacturing it doesn't seem like a job. I mean there are times when we're walking over the moors and I'm thinking 'This is it! I'm ... getting paid for this" (John, *Action for Youth*).

Not all was rosy, of course, and apart from the challenges posed by learners, which could make the job particularly stressful, a number of frustrations were evident. These included high workloads arising from the demands of target-driven approaches to teaching and managing the programme, the scarcity of work placements for learners, and the feeling that, because of the relatively short-term nature of E2E and a shortage of meaningful progression opportunities, the programme could be more about temporarily reducing NEET figures than transforming lives.

Much of the research into FE teacher identities and professionalism which took place following the traumas of incorporation points to feelings of downgraded status and dilemmas of resistance or compliance with respect to a new managerialism (Shain and Gleeson, 1999). Teachers in FE colleges, where cultural connections with pre-incorporation systems remained relatively strong for some time, experienced a sense of losing control over teaching and learning, and reductions in their sense of professionalism. Tutors in E2E programmes, particularly the younger or more recent entrants, have fewer cultural resources to draw on in constructing professional identities and in managing the interface between external pressures on teachers' status and autonomy and their own commitment to learners. Although the need for a delicate balancing act between managerial demands and the interests of teaching and learning is no less than for the FE teachers described by Avis and by Gleeson *et al* (2005), the sense of history and professionalism is perhaps less robust in E2E providers; this may explain why expressions of liberation and fulfilment figure so prominently in the accounts of the tutors in our research.

One of the greatest pressures on professional identities in FE teaching over the last twenty years has been the proliferation of teaching support roles in the sector, with job titles such as trainer, assessor and key worker. This has been partly due to a desire to reduce costs, transferring functions supposedly requiring less expertise from teachers to lower-paid support staff, but is also driven by the consequences of social inclusion policies and funding mechanisms which have led to the recruitment of younger and more vulnerable students (Gleeson *et al*, 2005). As we have seen, these support roles normally have lower qualification requirements, although in practice they may entail considerably more responsibility than their definition suggests.Even for staff still classed as teachers, the interaction between status and professional identity has been affected by these changes, and a shift from teacher as subject specialist to teacher as welfare officer is perceived by many in FE as part of a slow downgrading of professional status.

A central issue in our case-study sites was that E2E tutors were not regarded as teachers, and were referred to variously by terms such as tutor, trainer and key worker. More specialised roles also existed, such as E2E administrator and placement officer, which in spite of their names often entailed significant contact with learners.

> ... the last time I applied for a job, which was at *Aim for Work*, you didn't need a teaching qualification because the key worker role is not actually a teacher role and we are not classed as teachers which causes a controversy in this place because obviously most people here are teachers. So we don't get a teacher's wage; we're on support officer's scale. Whereas at *Aim for Work*,

where I worked before, I didn't need a teaching qualification but I wanted to have it because I knew that the way that the E2E was going to be developing I would need a teaching qualification eventually. (Susanna, Middlebridge College)

Pay and conditions were relatively poor compared with those for teachers in FE colleges and varied between individual providers. There were marked contrasts between the discourses of managers and practitioners, with managers tending to downplay staff turnover and differences in pay, whilst some practitioners felt that pay was a real issue. A Connexions PA who worked with a number of providers was quite explicit, saying that the frequent changes in staff were partly due to the stress of the job but also to 'massive' differences in pay and to staff not feeling valued. As we have seen, differences in pay and status were felt quite strongly at Middlebridge College, where tutors spoke of E2E being marginalised in organisational and curriculum terms.

Far from carrying out limited support roles, E2E staff had considerable autonomy in managing learning, and engaged in curriculum development for the new Foundation Learning programme planned to replace E2E in 2010. These tutors regarded themselves as no less professional than colleagues classed as teachers, but subject to much less favourable conditions: 'You have people doing 52 week contracts compared to teachers doing 40 week or 38 week contracts and the ones doing 52 week contracts are earning eight to ten grand less'. Ecclestone (2009) reports similar feelings and struggles over pay and status in E2E programmes in the south of England, where in one case E2E tutors had pressured college management into reviewing teaching roles.

In other providers, such contrasts were less evident and a significant feature was the flexibility of job roles and the ways in which non-teaching staff contributed to the experiences of young people (Thompson, 2010). Many roles involved contact with learners, and various staff could be involved in managing learner attendance, finding placements, and providing advice or pastoral support. In part, this sort of flexibility derives from the predominance of generic modes in the E2E curriculum (Simmons, 2009), in which everyday skills related to the contexts of life and work tend to reduce the status of teaching. However, it also appeared to open up the possibility of career development to staff who otherwise may not have aspired to a teaching role. We have already seen several cases where employment as a tutor followed from non-teaching posts or attending courses at providers; perhaps the most striking instance of this in our research was Leanne, a former E2E learner at *Aim for Work* who was currently working as an E2E administrator there. Leanne aspired eventually to become an E2E tutor and planned to take NVQs in Training and Development to help her achieve this aim.

Developing the E2E workforce?

Although routes to becoming an E2E tutor were complex and diverse, employment in this role almost invariably preceded any formal teacher training. For this reason, workforce development for E2E and similar programmes needs to encompass both some form of initial teacher training and continuing professional development. The question of professional development for these tutors is made more complex by the blurring of distinctions between teaching and welfare in E2E. Although, as we have already seen, the merging of these two roles is evident in FE generally, it is particularly acute in the case of work-based learning for young people, where the positioning of tutors as not quite teachers is widespread. In our case-study sites, professional knowledge appeared to be valued less than life experience, personal qualities and a sense of empathy for young people. Both tutors and managers employed similar discourses:

> I think it's a job where you either love it or you hate it. I don't think there is anything in between. The people we have are not teachers as such but, at the moment, they are all working towards teaching qualifications but they've all been out there in the workplace and they know what it's like and they all have a feeling for these young people. (Gillian, provider manager)

> I think there's a difference ... some people feel that if your teaching skills aren't as great ... it's treating people as individuals rather than as a group of faces. After years of that plus working in the other way as well you realise it's a different strategy and you have to adapt your strategies to suit your learner really and what we find with this client group is that the learner is teaching you as well. They'll show you the way even if they don't realise it themselves. (Steve, E2E tutor)

These distinctive characteristics of work-based learning for young people – and particularly the important formative role of workplace environments and cultures in framing the development of new tutors – must be taken into account when discussing professional development in contexts such as E2E. Furthermore, virtually all the professional development engaged in by E2E tutors is grounded in on-the-job experience, and is therefore itself a variety of work-based learning, albeit of the more general kind discussed in Chapter 1. As Orr and Simmons (2010) point out, 'the environment that trainees encounter is crucial to understanding what they learn ... about teaching'. However, recognising the importance of learning through informal and often mundane practices does not imply that it takes place in random ways outside social structures. Billett (2002) emphasises the cultural aspects of the experiences which contribute to learning in the workplace as follows:

> Workplace experiences are not informal. They are the product of the historical-cultural practices and situational factors that constitute the particular work practice, which in turn distributes opportunities for participation to individuals or cohorts of individuals. (p457)

Conceptualisations of workplace learning often begin from Lave and Wenger's (1991) notions of situated learning and communities of practice. In such models, apprenticeship and other modes of on-the-job training are seen as a linear progression from novice to expert, with a gradual and supported movement from the periphery – a place of limited responsibilities and guidance from more experienced colleagues – to the centre, where the former novice now plays a full role in the community of practice. However, Fuller and Unwin (2003) argue that this conceptualisation does not apply in many contemporary workplaces, where pressures for efficiency often require new employees to become fully productive as soon as possible. The novice may rapidly become a 'narrow expert', forced into a restrictive rather than expansive approach to learning and confining his or her development to coping with immediate organisational demands. Recognising these tensions, Fuller and Unwin introduce a framework based on an expansive-restrictive continuum, which has been used by a number of authors to analyse the workplace learning of tutors in FE colleges (Lucas and Unwin, 2009; Orr and Simmons, 2010) and in E2E programmes (Thompson, 2010).

In Fuller and Unwin's (2003) framework, an expansive approach to workforce development is characterised by a number of features that support the gradual development of a new employee and combine socialisation into the cultures and practices of a specific organisation with more broadly-based abilities and knowledge. This includes employer support in acquiring knowledge-based vocational qualifications which go beyond the immediate demands of the job, and recognition of the dual role of new employees as both learner and productive worker.

From the evidence of our research, this was not always the case. Although some managers acknowledged that FE workforce reforms and government aspirations for professionalisation would affect E2E providers, progress towards achieving the required qualification levels was patchy and irregular. As we have seen, rapid transitions from being a non-teaching employee to a full-time tutor were not unusual; together with new entrants recruited from industry and other occupations, and relatively high staff turnover in some providers, this continually supplied the staff base with new tutors requiring training.

Frequent movements of staff are a broader concern, and are not confined to our case-study sites. In 2008-09, approximately 75 per cent of staff in work-based learning providers had been employed there for less than three years (LLUK, 2010:4). Unsurprisingly, many tutors in our research had not yet completed their teaching qualifications, or were waiting to enrol on a course. Tara, a tutor at *Aim for Work*, commented that 'I've had a lot of coaching. I've not got the actual Cert Ed or PGCE or anything like that but I'm working towards it – or I will be working towards it by the end of this year'. The attitudes of managers towards the professionalisation agenda were ambivalent: although they spoke positively about the benefits for staff and learners, some were anxious about its implications for staff turnover:

> Everyone who is employed here needs to have or be working towards their PGCE or Cert Ed. Caroline [provider manager] says that the professionalisation of the workforce isn't necessarily a good thing as quite often they end up as a 'holding bay' for staff before they move on to better paid places of work. Many become teachers where they can earn more money. (Field notes, *MGC Training*)

Only Middlebridge College had a high proportion of tutors with full teaching qualifications; in other providers, the situation was sometimes contradictory and confusing. At *MGC Training*, for example, tutors without a full qualification were expected to be working towards a Cert Ed, PGCE or similar award. However, none of the tutors interviewed there had actually achieved the qualification, and only one was currently taking a course at this level. In some cases, there seemed to be tensions between the need for staff to become qualified and making sure that this actually happened:

> One of the first things I said when I was interviewed was that I wanted to be a college lecturer and I've been here for five years now and they've kept saying that my qualifications weren't the right ones. For a long time everything was up in the air so, in the end, three or four of us decided that we were just going to do it ourselves. (George, *Action for Youth* [quoted in Thompson, 2010])

In some cases, the positioning of tutors as not really teachers appeared to discourage them from working towards a teaching qualification, and tutors could themselves regard other areas of development as having greater relevance.

> I've done my assessor award when I first started because I didn't know which way I wanted to go – whether to be an assessor or a tutor. When I started you just went in and did it but last year I did my Learning and Development Level 3 but I'm not working towards a teacher's qualification. I think if I did anything it would be Advice and Guidance because that's mainly what I do. I do interviews and inductions and then progress them up ... (Sarah, *MGC Training*)

In such contexts, professional development of E2E tutors is likely to be driven more by instrumental concerns related to the practicalities of supporting learners, than a model of professionalism which takes a broader view of education, pedagogy and theory (Evans, 2008:26). Both at *MGC Training* and elsewhere, a number of tutors held teaching or training related qualifications at NVQ level 3, such as Training and Development, Learning and Development, and various assessor and verifier awards. In addition to teaching qualifications, tutors held vocationally-orientated qualifications, including NVQs related to the specialist focus of providers. Some were qualified in basic or key skills, counselling or careers guidance.

Of course, professionalism needs to be about much more than acquiring teaching qualifications. Professionalism, in any meaningful sense, cannot simply be created or imposed by external agencies, even governmental ones; it must be enacted in the practice of professionals (Evans, 2008) and their working conditions. As Thompson (2010) points out, policy, discourse and context are crucial factors influencing how professionalism is enacted in E2E. However, the indications from our research are that limited conceptualisations of learners and tutors combine to produce and reproduce restricted forms of professionalism and professional development. Perhaps even more than in FE colleges, the diverse entry routes and occupational backgrounds of practitioners leave them vulnerable to exploitation (Jephcote and Salisbury, 2009:971).

As we have seen earlier in this chapter, we found evidence of characteristic features of work intensification in the FE sector, such as an extended working year, demanding learner caseloads and being expected to perform tasks formerly undertaken by more senior or experienced staff (Mather *et al*, 2007). High turnover of staff and a relatively low proportion of tutors with full teaching qualifications were unlikely to encourage the development of the 'participative memory' described by Fuller and Unwin (2003:47) as assisting the process of acculturation in which less experienced tutors are drawn into a meaningful community of practice.

Tutors' constructions of E2E learners and learning

Learning is often presented as an individual act, something which takes place in the heads of learners and best conceptualised as a psychological process. However, there is a great deal to be gained by focusing on the ways in which learning is dependent on social interactions, both at the micro level (for example, between learners, between tutors, or between learner and tutor) and at the level of department, institution or educational system. From this perspective, learning is part of a set of social practices which strongly influence content, pedagogy and access.

In an influential study of learners and tutors in FE colleges, James and Biesta (2007) develop a cultural theory of learning, 'a theory which conceives of learning not as something which happens in the heads, minds or brains of students, but sees it as something that happens in and 'through' social practices' (p21). Drawing on the work of Pierre Bourdieu, they argue that the cultural context of learning is more than just a backdrop to educational experiences, and that learning is a cultural phenomenon in its own right. A learning culture is constituted by 'the social practices through which people learn' and in which the actions, dispositions and interpretations of participants are closely interwoven (James and Biesta, 2007:23).

Although all educational institutions enjoy a certain degree of autonomy, the learning culture of an institution cannot be separated from its positioning within the educational system as a whole. Learning in FE, as elsewhere in education, is affected by what Bourdieu calls 'the field of power'; that is, the dominant ruling structures in a society such as the state and its quasi-autonomous agencies. Thompson (2011b) discusses this point in relation to E2E.

The role of factors external to a particular learning site is therefore crucially important in the formation of a learning culture; government, funding agencies, employers and the perceptions of members of the public are all part of the field of external forces within which FE is positioned. To understand the learning cultures of E2E, therefore, the expressions and practices of tutors need to be related to the wider discourses and power relations around NEET young people discussed in earlier chapters.

As we have seen, young people attending E2E programmes form a heterogeneous group, and when tutors described their learners, many began with the statement: 'They're all different'. However, tutors identified a number of characteristics which they commonly encountered, corresponding broadly to the typologies of NEET young people discussed in earlier chapters. These included a lack of basic skills and low levels of self-esteem and motivation. Some learners had arrived with a history of behavioural or attendance issues at school or college, although tutors had not necessarily experienced this during the E2E programme:

> I think they're all different actually. It sounds awful but you can usually spot the ones you think are going to do quite well pretty early on ... those who come here at the beginning of July are the ones that go out on placement pretty quickly. Others take a long time to come through. I've got a lad here at the moment who has been on the programme for 32 weeks but from when he started to what he is now is amazing and probably a lot of it is not seen though we try to record it along the way – a lot of it is not seen. A lot of it is

about him coming out of his shell basically. The initial assessment that we got from his school said that he had behavioural issues and he tended to just fire off but it's never happened once. So I just sat down with him and discussed this and he said that when he was at school people used to wind him up but here he just got on with it. He never had an outburst here but he was just very, very quiet but he's fine now and he's one of those you can give a job to and you know he's going to do it. (George, *Action for Youth*)

The idea that E2E learners were difficult or challenging entailed contradictory and conflicting discourses; however, the increasing pastoral role which disrupted the professional identities of some FE tutors (Gleeson *et al*, 2005) was welcomed by most of the E2E staff interviewed. Indeed, for E2E tutors, providing close personal support within an ethos of care and nurture was an important part of their identity:

I don't see them as a challenge because you just take everybody as an individual. All you know about them is that they are disaffected but they could have personal problems stopping them moving on to positive outcomes like employment or further education. That's where the pastoral side comes in and that's why the role is split in half. I think it's a good split because you feel that you have more time to spend with them than you would if you were a full-time course tutor. (Fran, Middlebridge College [quoted in Thompson, 2010])

They are very demanding learners I would say. They come with a lot of issues and some come and just get on with it, some are just undecided and that's why they are on E2E but they are academically capable, but you've also got the other learners who come with a lot of baggage and they've got housing issues; social issues such as domestic violence; some are attending counselling sessions and what not. So they are very challenging but that's our job. (Sarah, *Action for Youth* [quoted in Thompson, 2010])

Perhaps the most distinctive element of the learning cultures in our case-study sites was a discourse which constructed learners as unable to cope with written work and, by implication, to learn successfully in formal settings. Some of the practices associated with this discourse have already been discussed in Chapter 5, together with the assumptions and weaknesses of adopting such a position in relation to a highly diverse group of learners. Apart from a widespread propensity to employ discourses of the non-academic E2E learner – what Thomson and Russell (2009) refer to as constructing learners as a homogeneous group, 'good with their hands, not with their heads', most tutors tried to avoid stereotypes – the emphasis on difference was one strategy they used to do this. Words such as 'disadvantaged' and 'underprivileged' were used with caution, although at times there were references to 'types' of learner and it was said that tutors developed a sixth sense by which they could distinguish an E2E learner from other young people. Expectations of learners could be strongly modified by the experience of working on the programme, with some tutors talking about a 'reality check' which made them realise that the power of E2E to change the lives of young people was severely limited. The frustrations of combining encouragement with pragmatism were acutely felt, particularly in the face of learners whose basic skills were so limited that their aspirations for vocational training seemed a long way from being fulfilled:

> It's about getting them to realise that doing anything work-wise they'll need their basic skills because there are a lot more people better equipped than they are to get a job ... We had a lad recently and he was totally convinced that he was going to be an electrician and we tried to explain to him that his basic skills weren't good enough and that he needed to work on certain skills but he wasn't prepared to do that ... But some people come here and they will put the hard work into the basic skills part of it so they can get on to a course at college. They have the practical ability but they need the basic skills. (George, *Action for Youth*)

Although the likelihood of learners achieving their aims in the relatively near future was often low, a central feature of the E2E learning culture was a set of practices and discourses which valorised progress in personal effectiveness and employability, weaving together perceptions of moving on from earlier failure and challenging circumstances. As noted in Chapter 5, posters and other displays produced by students or tutors told stories of what could be achieved through E2E, of successful learners and the opportunities for employment or training to which learners could aspire. Individualised target-setting and regular reviews of progress encouraged young people to identify and celebrate what they had achieved and look ahead to further successes. In general, tutors found these processes helpful; although time-consuming, they were felt to be part of the intensive personal support for learners intended to be a focus of E2E.

A learner might have problems with time keeping so we will set them targets to arrive on time every day for a week ... Little steps can lead to bigger ones. It's important for them to have targets to meet because it gives them a purpose ...They are not ridiculous targets. So, for example, if they are working in a childcare environment you might say to a learner: 'For your first week try to learn the names of the staff you are working with and what they do or the names of the children'. Or the target might be: 'Read this story to the classroom'. (Jenny, *MGC Training* [quoted in Thompson, 2010])

For the young people involved, the usefulness of targets was not widely appreciated, and they tended to talk in terms of filling in forms or being told what to do next. Such feelings of passivity and being on the receiving end of an external agenda were not unusual, and parallel the experiences of some NEET young people when dealing with professionals. For example, Hoggarth and Smith (2004:14) highlight the negative reactions from young people brought about when Connexions PAs appeared not to listen to expressed needs or to exert pressure to take up particular options. Nevertheless, most E2E learners interviewed placed a high value on the individualised support available from practitioners and used a similar discourse of progression to tutors.

Ecclestone (2009) remarks on the 'invisibility' of structural conditions as a significant part of the learning culture in E2E. To some extent, this is inevitable in that it was difficult for tutors to challenge some of the forces involved. Relations of class, gender and ethnicity alongside structural conditions in the economy were clearly important, and were recognised by some tutors. In spite of a tendency to overestimate the influence of individual characteristics, tutors in the case-study sites were well aware of external realities and the highly competitive environment that learners would face on leaving the programme. Some learning activities enabled broader social issues to be discussed, for example by using EMA as a focus in literacy sessions (Russell *et al*, 2011) and the discussion of multiculturalism touched on in the field note extract in Chapter 5. Explicit critique of capitalist relations was almost entirely absent from the discourse of tutors although, as we saw in the previous chapter, some tutors claimed to deal honestly with learners over the matter of work placements. Nevertheless, in daily interactions between tutors and learners, awareness of structures tended to be set aside as a pragmatic response to immediate issues. The predominant approach to gaining the confidence and trust of learners and motivating them to engage in the work required was to highlight an individualised response based on promised rewards for completing E2E. These benefits included greater personal effectiveness, enhanced CVs, relevant vocational qualifications and the chance of progressing to further education or employment.

> Mainly I would say the one thing that they have in common is that they need a little help with their maths and English and a little bit of motivation – but not necessarily everyone. I think they just need a little bit of direction and a little bit of help just to tell them that it's not such a scary world out there and we can help them to get a job. We help them put CVs together and do job search and things like that. It's a more grown up style of learning, I think. But, on the whole, I think they are all different and it's difficult to say there is one type because they have so many different backgrounds. (Jenny, *MGC Training* [quoted in Thompson, 2010])

It was rare to encounter more than passive resistance to this discourse amongst learners, and many embraced it wholeheartedly.

> ... we're building up our folder at the moment and it's got, like, our CV and we've done our health and safety and I was supposed to do my First Aid but I missed it. So we're just building our folder up and you get, like, your number skills and everything ... It's sort of like another qualification really. It guarantees you onto another course because it ensures that you've got First Aid and health and safety and you've got your CV and whatnot so you're not just going in with nothing. So you could have a couple of people going onto a course and one might have school GCSEs and another person coming in from an E2E course with health and safety, First Aid and his folder full of things. (Patrick, Middlebridge College [quoted in Russell *et al*, 2011])

Discourse plays an important part in shaping the specific form of a learning culture; however, as Biesta and James point out, material forces within and external to learning sites also have a significant impact. The degree of autonomy possessed by educational institutions depends on their accumulation of material capital as well as cultural and social varieties; in the context of E2E, all of these are limited, partly by the fragmented biographies and histories of tutors and providers, but also by the material relations in which the programme is embedded. Although it was clear that discourses of employability were significant in shaping the practice within case-study sites, funding mechanisms based on qualifications achieved (Wolf, 2011) and a *quid pro quo* which could benefit employers who provided placements were also important factors:

> To support E2E requires a great deal of ... human resource and you've got some providers who are public companies and, therefore, they want a profit margin and you've got others who are charitable organisations so the amount of support they give to those young people means that they are not actually receiving as much money as they need to cover it so ... one of the key questions would be [whether] every young person received a one hundred per cent individualised programme ... because of the human resource element and the funding it's not always possible to do that for all young people ... (Partnership Manager)

> We've actually got a few new placements which have luckily come on board at the right time ... we'll go out and speak to the employers about the E2E programme and try and sell it to them. Basically the opportunity for them is that we will pay for the learners' training so, for instance, if they want to go into warehousing we will try and get them an FLT [fork-lift truck] licence ... We tend to ask for [the employer's] support with it as well because we can't afford it all but we do support the young person. (Tara, *Aim for Work*)

Although some learners had spent substantial periods of time on the programme, there was constant pressure to find what were regarded as positive progression outcomes – for example, employment with training or further education – within six months or so. Again, material as well as discursive relations contributed to this pressure, through funding arrangements, constraints on numbers, and quality assurance mechanisms. In one provider (not one of our case-study sites), practitioners recounted how managers had attempted to maximise learner numbers, conflicting with a later decision by the Learning and Skills Council to cap learner numbers. In addition to causing what they described as 'gridlock' across the partnership, the cap created a funding gap in this particular provider; as a result, two learners were told to leave the E2E programme – an unhappy task which fell to a tutor and a Connexions Personal Adviser (see Russell *et al*, 2010).

Working with parents?

There is strong evidence that demonstrates the influence of parents on the attitudes of young people towards education and training, even beyond compulsory school age (Payne, 2003). Ball, Maguire and Macrae

(2000) highlight social class differences in the ways that parents help to frame the aspirations of their children, and Mann (1998) shows that, for working-class girls in post-16 education, mother-daughter relationships are particularly important. However, Thompson (2011b) argues that parents and carers of young people attending E2E programmes occupy an anomalous position in relation to the perceived nature of their role and the legitimacy of their interest in the participation of their children.

In most areas of post-16 education in England, marketisation has led to providers such as colleges and sixth-forms positioning parents alongside their children as consumers. Parents' evenings, open days and regular contact between providers and parents are commonplace for young people in the more elite parts of the post-compulsory education system. By contrast, the parents of E2E learners are discursively positioned as part of the problems facing young people, and may have limited involvement in the decisions affecting them. Some practitioners conceptualised learners as from 'families that have gone off the rails ... from sink estates' and expressed low expectations of parents, for example, 'This type of young person has very little parental involvement' (Thompson, 2011b:24). When combined with concerns expressed by tutors over confidentiality, developing the independence of young people and the appropriateness of close parental involvement for post-16 learners, such conceptualisations led to a powerful set of discourses tending to exclude parents.

> We don't have parents evening, no. I think because we are trying to teach them to be independent we try not to involve the parents really. Again it depends on where you are and who you're dealing with. Sometimes parents want to know and sometimes, unfortunately, the parents are not involved in the learner's life. And we get the odd few who literally live on their own so there isn't any parental involvement there at all. But we don't try and get the parents involved unless the learners want us to. (Susanna, Middlebridge College)

Thompson (2011b) sees the exclusionary discourses and practices adopted by practitioners in relation to parents as part of their construction of what Bourdieu calls a 'legitimate authority', establishing the expertise and personal qualities of practitioners in contradistinction to both the chaotic lives and lack of interest of parents and the remoteness of schoolteachers. Parents of E2E learners were positioned as unpredictable and displaying contradictory and inappropriate behaviours, some being excessively deferential to practitioners and unwilling to engage in constructive dialogue, whilst others were described as unable to maintain self-control in meetings. For example, a Connexions PA described one parent as screaming at her son, and others automatically agreeing with tutors when disputes arose. One tutor explained that she received parental feedback only 'very rarely', and although apparently happy to respond to enquiries she did not actively encourage them (Thompson, 2011b:24).

> Sometimes what's happened is parents have brought them to the interview because they've not had confidence to come on their own and in that case they will ring up and tell us that they are concerned because they tell you their concerns at the interview. But what I always say is that if the young person agrees that their parents can ring up then that is fine and if a parent rings up to ask about their child I will always say can I get back to you because I will then go out and find the young person and tell them that their parent has rung up and did they want me to speak to them. Because they are post-16. So we don't get a lot of feedback from parents and we try not to get them involved too much because we would be answerable to every single parent about everything then.

Another Connexions PA expressed similar views:

> Some of the parents do engage but that's very rare but some parents do have an input and they might ring up to say that their child won't be in today ... or they might ring you up because they've got a trouble or need some information. But, again, the parents will always blame somebody else as well; it's never their fault. [Quoted in Thompson, 2011a]

Parental involvement was often considered inappropriate for post-16 learners and confidentiality was cited as an inhibiting factor. This was particularly the case for Connexions PAs, who sometimes received information from learners that would not have been disclosed if the young person thought it may be passed on.

> I think this is a tricky one – because of the age of the students confidentiality is an issue. If they are under sixteen you would tell the parents' but actually we don't require the parents consent. But sometimes we will get phone calls from a parent who has a question and it's mostly around the EMA I must admit. (Connexions PA)

164

In other circumstances, some practitioners welcomed parental interest, regarding it as indicating support at home, and also as an opportunity to obtain background information or to work with parents in keeping young people engaged with the programme. Contact with parents was seen as a way of informing them about the nature of E2E and countering misconceptions, although on some occasions this could result in parents displaying more enthusiasm than their children:

> [A few parents come to the interview] – especially now with the schools coming on to E2E we will get a lot of the learners come with parents or grandparents and occasionally an older brother or sister. But you do your spiel and whoever has brought the young person will say: 'I think I'll come here!' and that happens all the time and the young person is walking behind with a face as long as a wet weekend and showing no interest at all. Or if a parent or a grandparent comes with them ... they will say they thought it were really good and they will encourage the learner to get involved. But if they come on their own they'll go home and the parents will say: 'Well, how did it go?' 'It were alright.' 'So what did you do?' 'All sorts' ... I do sometimes get parents ringing up saying: 'what is it that you do?' because they don't know and asking their son is like pulling teeth. (Gillian, Provider Manager)

Thompson (2011b) emphasises that such practices do not imply that practitioners consciously seek to exclude parents, and attributes them to the forces operating within the Bourdieuian field of E2E provision. Within a field of struggles for authority between competing groups 'there is a production of difference which is in no way the product of a *search for* difference' (Bourdieu and Wacquant, 1992:100, original emphasis). Effectively, parents are discursively positioned within this field as occupying the same deficit category as their children, and are afforded little legitimate authority. The structuring of perceptions and dispositions provided by the field creates a learning culture which has for parents only a marginal place.

7

Conclusion: what does research say to policy?

We hope this book provides valuable insights into the experiences of marginalised learners, and will help practitioners and policymakers consider how best to engage these young people. But we have not intended to set out some sort of guide or blueprint for best practice. We do, however, believe that research has an important role to play in challenging some of the more entrenched and inaccurate assumptions about young people that infiltrate not only political discourse, but also public opinion and commonsense assumptions about social life more generally (France, 2007:165). In the spirit of C. Wright-Mills' (1959) belief that social science should engage with wider public debate, we have contested widely held misconceptions about education, work and social change, and questioned many of the underlying assumptions of state discourse. We have sought to offer alternative conceptions of young people on the margins of education and training. In this chapter, we draw together the main themes of the book and review its arguments and findings. We reflect on the lives and ambitions of NEET young people, the learning experiences provided for them, and the work of practitioners.

The book concludes by considering alternative approaches to engaging and re-engaging NEET young people. This, we argue, would require not only re-thinking interventions but also making comprehensive changes in the way society and economy is ordered. However, before considering the implications of our findings, it is important to place this work in the broader context of how educational research is received, used and evaluated. The chapter begins, therefore, by discussing different approaches to this question, and their relationship to wider social and economic issues.

The notions of policy science and policy scholarship provide a useful framework for considering the nature and purpose of educational research (Ball, 1995; Avis, 2006). *Policy science* focuses upon using research to improve practice – or how practice can be made more efficient and effective. This perspective implies that educational research should be regarded as an applied social science (Anderson, 1990), underpinned by the assumption that education is the key to social mobility. This position is rooted in neo-liberal interpretations of the purpose of education and linked to notions such as *good practice, best practice*, and other attempts to identify and prescribe the most effective approaches to teaching and learning. Whilst successive governments in the UK and elsewhere have increasingly called for research that is *evidence-based*, education policy in the West has reflected the dominant neo-liberal ideology. Consequently, research findings tend to be deemed useful only where they confirm pre-conceived conclusions, and education policy is often made without a robust evidential base. It is often designed and implemented despite research suggesting potentially more fruitful alternatives. As we saw in Chapter 2, education policy in the UK and elsewhere is driven largely by normative assumptions about globalisation and economic competitiveness, and takes place against the backdrop of broader neo-liberal beliefs about human nature.

Educational research encounters distinctive forms of pressure for academics to demonstrate the utility of their work. During the 1980s, educational research was criticised for its lack of relevance to practitioners and policymakers; generally, it was also viewed by government as expensive, of poor quality and politicised. These concerns intensified under successive New Labour governments (Harris, 2007:115-116) and, although some factions within the Coalition Government have been more equivocal, there is nevertheless growing pressure to align educational research more closely with the perceived needs of teachers, policymakers, and business. Furthermore, certain currents within the academic community advocate the need for closer links between research and practitioner needs (Tooley and Darby, 1998; CERI, 2002).

Indeed, the general public often assumes that the purpose of educational research is directly to inform practice. To be fair, it is important to recognise that practitioners can sometimes draw on academic research to inform and improve their work. Some research is intended specifically for this purpose, and this is often valid and worthwhile. However, not all educational research takes this form, despite the current fashion for impact. Concentrating merely on *what works* or what offers *best value* leaves little space for broader intellectual or moral questions about the aims and purpose of education (Harris, 2007:135).

We recognise that there is a place for research which examines the work of practitioners and aims to help develop educational systems and practices. However, research which focuses purely on classroom practice is likely to overlook a range of other important factors which affect educational outcomes, both for individual students and for society more generally. Educational success and failure are complex, socially constructed processes dependent upon a range of tightly intertwined social, cultural, economic and institutional factors. Furthermore, despite repeated assertions by the major political parties about the key role of education in promoting social mobility, the possibility of this is limited unless broader inequalities are tackled.

As we have explained in this book, the main beneficiaries of rising educational standards and increased levels of participation have been from the higher social classes. Such observations lead towards more critical conceptions of the nature and purpose of educational research. In contrast to policy science, *policy scholarship* seeks to place research within its wider social and economic context and views education as a site of struggle. Although the findings of policy scholarship may not always be immediately applicable to the classroom, the structuring and constraining effects of social and economic relations, and the internal contradictions within policy formulation, must be legitimate concerns for educational research.

Advocates of instrumental research such as Tooley and Darby (1998) regard policy scholarship as too distanced from practice to be valuable. For them, research should be aimed directly at the practitioner, rather than burdened with sociological or philosophical debates. Such matters, it is argued, are only likely to obscure and reduce the utility of research findings, and the ability of practitioners to apply the recommendations flowing from them.

Avis (2006) criticises this stance on a number of grounds. Whilst he acknowledges that research claiming to be objective, value-free and directly related to action may appeal to some, he argues that policy science approaches tend to over-simplify complex social phenomena. Ultimately, the desire for immediacy may descend to the level of tips-for-teachers, isolated from critical awareness of the social antagonisms and inequalities surrounding educational processes.

However, whilst the notions of policy science and policy scholarship offer a certain heuristic value, it is often difficult to classify research as falling entirely into one camp or the other. Many concerned with improving practice have a strong sense of structural inequality and an affinity with critical pedagogy. Consequently, it is perhaps best to regard the relationship between policy science and policy scholarship as a continuum rather than a sharp divide.

NEET discourse and progressive practice

Whilst the direction and purpose of education and training is driven, to a large extent, by social and economic change and the priorities of policymakers, practitioners are not without agency. Rarely do they simply transfer policy decisions into the classroom or workshop in a straightforward or uncritical fashion. Indeed, educationalists have an important role to play in mediating and sometimes subverting policy, and there is a long tradition of practitioner resistance and progressive practice in working with marginalised learners.

For example, in the 1980s, Gleeson (1983) highlighted how tutors working with young people on youth training schemes were often able to engage in creative practice despite the constraints of such programmes. Similarly, Ainley (1990) has explained how, during the same period, teachers were able to subvert Keith Joseph's attempt to reintroduce a technical stream into schools, the Technical and Vocational Education Initiative (TVEI). Although TVEI was intended to be utilitarian and competence-based in nature, in many cases practitioners were able to use the additional funding attached to the programme to develop and implement imaginative new activities with their students.

In our E2E research, we found the practice of tutors and Connexions PAs to be bounded by structural and material factors, as well as the discourses surrounding NEET young people. However, they often recognised the complex needs and circumstances of young people: although many learners were challenging to engage, practitioners were normally caring and concerned about their welfare. Generally, we found E2E tutors to be enthusiastic and committed to learner progression. Whilst the flexible nature of programmes such as E2E can sometimes cause organisational and logistical difficulties, we found that E2E tutors could exploit this flexibility and find space to work with young people in constructive ways. It remains to be seen how practitioners will navigate the more structured and arguably more restrictive replacement for E2E, Foundation Learning.

In order to develop our argument it will be useful to think about what we mean by progressive practice. We recognise that the practitioner's role in working with marginalised and disadvantaged young people includes helping learners to build self-esteem and personal effectiveness. Many young people attending provision such as E2E have had negative educational experiences, and some enter programmes having significant personal issues and barriers to learning. As such, it is important to acknowledge that a nurturing and caring approach to pedagogy can be valid and necessary (Hyland, 2009). However, NEET young people should not be pathologised. Emphasising nurturing at the expense of intellectual challenge is limiting and, in many ways, inadequate. Denying access to coherent, principled knowledge in order to concentrate on building generic, transferable skills and dispositions is problematic. There are, after all, only so many times a young person can update a CV or improve their interview skills before an unavoidable conclusion is reached: that is, coherent skills and knowledge need to be gained in order to add substance to any inter-personal abilities that have been accrued.

Some practitioners regarded E2E learners as fundamentally different to other young people, particularly in their dispositions towards conceptual learning and traditional forms of educational practice. Because learners were generally seen as non-academic, great emphasis was placed upon what was deemed to be a work-related curriculum. Provision was based largely upon building confidence and personal and social effectiveness alongside the acquisition of narrow vocational competencies. In our view, progressive practice includes a critical pedagogy which challenges dominant discourses about the inherently problematic nature of NEET young people, and questions the causes of inequality. It should expose learners to principled, conceptual knowledge – as well as providing a supportive environment. Generally, learners were positioned as requiring personal interventions rather than knowledge and skills. On entry to E2E, this may well be true, and the disrupted educational histories and personal difficulties of many learners have been amply documented in earlier chapters. However, the limited duration of E2E, and the imperative to move learners on as quickly as possible to demonstrate progression, means that providing a sound basis for sustainable outcomes can come a poor second to targets and funding constraints. Consequently, young people leaving E2E programmes were highly likely to return to NEET status within a relatively short time. Indeed, during our research E2E was one of the major sources of new entrants to the NEET category.

At this point it is worth re-stating some characteristics of the young people who took part in the project, and re-emphasising that learners on E2E and similar programmes form a varied and diverse group of young people, with a broad range of experience and abilities. Whilst many learners on E2E programmes in Greenford and Middlebridge had spent periods being NEET, half had experience of paid work; only a quarter had no GCSE passes, and nearly half had at least one GCSE at grade C or above. Virtually all the young people had aspirations for work or further education, and some had ambitions to go on to higher education or professional study. The young people taking part in our research did not appear to be part of an entrenched workless underclass. We found no evidence of fecklessness or an ingrained dependency. More than 80 per cent of the young people on the E2E programmes we studied were from households with at least one parent in paid employment. Moreover, those from families without work were not from households without a history of employment. Far from being drawn from an underclass with antisocial attitudes and an antipathy to work, the young people we came across in the course of our research were essentially ordinary people from families not dissimilar from working-class learners in more mainstream provision. These learners were from ordinary backgrounds with everyday attitudes and ambitions which included obtaining employment and other signifiers of adult life (Russell *et al*, 2011).

Engaging learners attending programmes such as E2E is often difficult, and our point about the nature of the curriculum and the type of learning that NEET young people are offered presents some thorny issues. The nature of the pedagogy to which learners are exposed is dependent on a range of factors, but perhaps most immediately, the curriculum design and the qualities of practitioners are important influences upon young people and their progress, both educationally and socially. Whilst we found many positive features of teaching and learning on the E2E programmes we studied, it was also clear that tutor professionalism was restricted in a variety of ways. Generally, E2E tutors were poorly paid in comparison to those teaching in mainstream education. They were paid significantly less than schoolteachers and, in some cases, less than their colleagues working in other parts of the FE system. Although some were graduates and held formal teaching qualifications, many E2E tutors had not undertaken extensive post-compulsory education. Moreover, their professional development rested largely on individual motivation and personal circumstances. Many had become tutors as a result of personal and local connections; informal routes into work were commonplace for tutors working on E2E programmes (Thompson, 2010). We found a significant degree of staff turnover amongst E2E providers in Greenford and Middlebridge. If we are serious about improving the learning opportunities available to marginalised young people, there are clearly important issues to consider.

Staff recruitment and retention strategies, rates of pay, and structured and transparent career pathways all need to be addressed if NEET young people are to receive consistently high-quality learning programmes. Furthermore, if young people are to be provided with access to coherent and principled forms of knowledge, staff responsible for teaching and learning need to possess the necessary knowledge and skills to enable this to take place. Tutors need to be especially skilful practitioners in order to devise challenging yet accessible learning opportunities in a range of contexts. Access to ongoing professional development which provides both knowledge and skills-based learning opportunities is particularly important for those working with learners on the margins of participation.

This leads to a further conclusion: providing NEET young people with meaningful learning experiences requires not only a more sophisticated understanding of the social matrix within which their learning takes place, it also needs to be funded in a way that supports practitioner development and enables programmes to meet the needs of learners for sustainable outcomes. This, in turn, leads us to broader questions not only about how various forms of education and training are resourced but also about our priorities as a society.

Employment, economy and social justice

Since the financial crisis of 2008, policymakers across the western world, but perhaps especially in the UK, have repeatedly emphasised the requirement for austerity and the urgent need to reduce public expenditure. This time, we are told, there really is no alternative. This is, of course, not the case. Governments are not powerless in the face of globalisation; economies can be managed and attempts to tackle inequality can be made. Rates of taxation, whether these are personal or corporation taxes, can be made progressive and equitable. For the last thirty years at least, official discourse has promoted neo-liberal understandings, not just of the economy but increasingly of all social relations. In the UK, the current Conservative-Liberal Democrat coalition offers an undiluted neo-liberal agenda; any commitment to social justice offered by their New Labour predecessors – however shallow this was – has been abandoned. Despite the fact that the global economic crisis, and the meltdown of the banking system in particular, was caused by free market ideology and business-oriented policy decisions, apparently the key to future prosperity lies in market individualism. The prime minister has pledged to commission public service provision from private and voluntary sector providers wherever possible, rather than direct public service delivery (Cameron, 2011). Yet clearly there are alternative, and arguably more effective and efficient, ways of organising not only education and training systems but society at large.

The effects of neo-liberalism are felt unevenly across society. Certain individuals and groups are systematically advantaged whilst others are disempowered by the prevailing political climate. For young people, the consequences of the latest economic downturn have been profound. Most immediately, it is clear that the sharp increase in unemployment and underemployment caused by the latest recession has had a disproportionately large effect on young people (Bell and Blanchflower, 2010). However, it is important to re-emphasise that social class has a strong mediating effect upon life chances, and that these differences are intensified and exacerbated by conditions of economic crisis. For the lowest-achieving young people, particularly those from working-class backgrounds, their options consist mainly of low-status training schemes with little labour-market value, casual, part-time low grade work or unemployment. For many in this position, leaving school is followed by churning between forms of participation, punctuated by periods of being NEET.

Youth transitions today are more individualised than they were for much of the twentieth century but they continue to be closely related to structural inequality. Undoubtedly, there has been a breakdown of the stable pathways and predictable biographies connected to class and community that characterised the post-war decades, and many of these changes can be interpreted positively. Many young people embrace the notion of creating their own identity, and the sometimes claustrophobic cultures of post-war England should not be romanticised. But, whilst some of the constraints which limited the horizons of many young people may well have diminished, this should not be confused with emancipation or equality. Structured inequalities continue to exist and in some ways have intensified (Bynner, 2005). They are, however, now perceived and interpreted individually rather than collectively. Young people are cut off from previous forms of identity and collective support mechanisms (Beck and Beck-Gernsheim, 2002). They are forced to participate in new forms of decision-making, and to create their own pathways and futures.

Whilst educational and labour market inequalities are characteristic of capitalist economies in general, the commercialisation and marketisation of education systems intensifies the advantages enjoyed by privileged groups at the expense of the less fortunate (Ball, 2003). Young working-class people are confronted by a range of options often not well understood by them or their families (Yates *et al*, 2010). NEET young people may lack certain forms of social and cultural capital, and the practical support mechanisms, necessary to exercise informed choice in the educational marketplace. They are particularly vulnerable to the turbulent policy environment and vicissitudes of funding under which training providers operate (Russell *et al*, 2010). Whilst improving learning opportunities for NEET young people is of great importance, a policy environment which emphasises competition and insecurity will disadvantage them systematically in comparison to those taking part in high status forms of learning. These observations lead us towards a broader consideration of vocational education and its relationship to broader social and economic issues.

Re-thinking learning

The recent Wolf Review (2011) indicates that many young people accrue little labour market value from low-level vocational qualifications. It identifies formal academic qualifications, such as GCSEs, in English and mathematics as the credentials most fundamental to future success. We regard this as an important if unsurprising finding. Whilst there has always been prejudice against certain forms of vocational learning, especially in England (Hyland and Winch, 2007), the intrinsic value offered by the explanatory power contained within a knowledge-based curriculum must be recognised. It is this power which, we argue, needs to be made accessible to all those capable of benefiting from it. The challenge for those responsible for planning, designing and delivering the curriculum for marginalised learners is how to marry the practical and the theoretical in imaginative and accessible ways. Whilst work-based and vocational learning can open up opportunities, the skills and aptitudes gained on such programmes need to be underpinned by conceptual knowledge – knowledge which enables learners to see past discrete, atomised work-related tasks, and to make connections between the workplace and the outside world in a critical and coherent fashion.

The Wolf Review makes a number of useful observations about the structure and content of vocational education in England, and many of its recommendations are of value. For example, the proposal that vocational students continue to study a core of academic subjects alongside their main programme of study, including English and mathematics, is helpful. Similarly, we support Wolf's view that the system of funding post-16 education and training should be reformed. The current system which encourages providers to shift learners away from challenging but valuable courses onto low-level provision with little labour market value is deeply problematic. However, despite many useful observations, the Wolf Review is limited by its restricted remit. In our view, by concentrating mainly on the structure and content of vocational qualifications, the report focuses too heavily on supply-side issues.

Whilst such matters are important, they are only part of the equation when considering the efficacy of vocational education. Although Wolf acknowledges a problem with the demand for skills, tangible measures to address this situation were beyond the scope of the review. The Wolf Review therefore avoids an elephant in the room: many employers do not require high levels of skill from their workers. This is a significant shortfall. Whilst pockets of high-skill employment exist in the UK, this is not typical of the economy in general. The harsh reality is that the UK relies increasingly on relatively low-paid and localised service sector employment and low-cost, low-specification goods and services which can be afforded by those on low incomes, either at home or abroad. Whilst academic research has shown the low level of demand for skill to be highly problematic, policymakers have, in the main, overlooked this matter:

> Because, in general, employers in Britain make relatively few demands on workers in terms of skills it is unsurprising that consequently there is relatively little demand for skills training. Thus, it could be argued that, for skills, it is a lack of demand rather than supply that is the problem. However, despite this, governments ... have resolutely refused to tackle the relatively low levels of demand for skills... (Simmons, 2008:431)

The creation of more skilled employment would have two benefits: firstly, it would make participation in education and training more attractive to those who currently lack qualifications and experience, as the labour market value of qualifications would be enhanced. Secondly, by absorbing those with relatively high qualification levels who currently occupy intermediate-level jobs, it would make space in the labour market for relatively inexperienced and less well-qualified young people.

Rather than attempting to intervene in labour or product markets, successive governments have chosen to focus almost exclusively on supply-side issues. On the one hand, there have been various attempts to expand the available pool of labour. Increased levels of immigration, the encouragement of women to return to work after having children, and moves to raise the retirement age are some of the most obvious examples of this. Measures to increase the volume of labour have been accompanied by benefits restrictions aimed at creating a more flexible workforce ready to accept part-time, temporary and insecure work. On the other hand, there has been a pervasive discourse emphasising the priority of education and workforce skills as the key to employability, prosperity and social well-being – despite little evidence for the economic benefits of many qualifications.

In the UK, over 30 years of neo-liberalism have resulted in a society more unequal, more divided and less socially mobile than at any time since before the inter-war period. There has been a systematic empowerment of the rich, not only through taxation and inheritance laws but also by restructuring public services, and the valorisation of individualism, entrepreneurialism and capital more generally. The wealthiest twenty per cent have a significantly greater share of post-tax income in the UK than in 1979, whilst the poorest section of society has seen its share of income decline substantially (Byrne, 2005:95-96). Alongside this there has been a conscious reduction of the power and organisation of the working-class and the institutions which traditionally represented them. The position of NEET young people in contemporary society needs to be understood within this context: patterns of participation, inclusion and exclusion cannot be adequately explained within a discourse of individualised deficit. They derive to a significant degree from policies actively pursued by the state. This becomes clear when alternative responses to globalisation and social change are considered.

Policy choices made by the UK's long-standing economic rival, Germany, offer an interesting contrast and reference point from which to view matters of employment, training and workplace skills. During the first decade of the 21st century levels of unemployment in Germany appeared relatively high in comparison to many other western nations and the UK in particular. Received wisdom blamed excessive labour market regulation and rigidity as significant causes of Germany's plight (Barysch, 2003). In contrast, the UK's highly flexible labour market was congratulated by neo-liberal discourse as creating employment, and as

178

helping to keep levels of unemployment low. Extensive labour market deregulation, institutional reform and welfare retrenchment were deemed necessary to cure German unemployment (Erlinghagen and Knuth, 2010:87).

Subsequent events have shown the tenuous nature of such normative assumptions. The UK's highly flexible labour market has not prevented substantial rises in unemployment since the economic crisis of 2008, particularly amongst young people. Meanwhile, unemployment in Germany is now significantly below that of most comparable nations, and its economic growth far exceeds that of the UK.

There are a number of possible explanations for this, but perhaps we should begin by explaining that headline rates of unemployment can be deceptive. Like other statistics, unemployment figures are social constructs, and there are important variations in the way that different governments create and compile unemployment figures. Consequently, international comparisons are difficult. Nevertheless, German unemployment rates are more likely to include greater numbers of jobless people than is the case in France and Denmark, for example, where those without work are more likely to be classified as disabled, as retired, or as carers than as unemployed. This trend is even more marked in countries with strongly neo-liberal regimes, such as the UK (Erlinghagen and Knuth, 2010). Viewed in this light, the problem of German unemployment was always perhaps something of a mirage.

There are more tangible reasons for the relative success of the German economy. In part, these differences derive from deep-rooted differences between the two nations – for example, in attitudes towards technology, research and development, and different forms of education and training. Recent policy decisions in both nations have increased polarisation between them. Whereas successive governments have allowed much of the UK's traditional industrial base to collapse, state intervention in Germany has encouraged a greater degree of continuity and enabled much of the country's production industry to survive and flourish. Furthermore, there have been significant differences in business strategy between the two nations.

Whilst the UK economy continues to be trapped in a *low skills equilibrium* (Finegold and Soskice, 1988), far more German companies have chosen to aim at high-quality, high-value product markets. This difference is not accidental; in Germany, state policy promotes the demand for skill rather than focusing disproportionately on supply. A significant characteristic of German labour markets is the widespread use of compulsory licences to practice across many sectors of employment. Although such requirements exist in a few professions in the UK, they are widespread in Germany. There are also significant differences in education and training between the two nations. Whilst vocational learning in the UK has always been regarded as inferior to academic and general education, in Germany, it has tended to be more highly regarded (Hyland and Winch, 2007). This is reflected in higher levels of funding allocated to vocational training, and the more rigorous and extensive content of these programmes in Germany in comparison to those found in the UK.

If we are serious about engaging and re-engaging NEET young people, a shift in their conceptualisation is necessary. Rather than regarding disengagement as an illness to be cured or a condition to be rectified, it would be more apposite to see youth unemployment and social exclusion more generally as deriving from conscious policy decisions made within a neo-liberal context. There is a range of possible options that could help improve the position of young people outside education, employment and training. Some of these relate to the provision offered to them, and we believe that implementing the suggestions earlier in this chapter would be worthwhile. More broadly, we also welcome the current Government's proposal to expand the number of apprenticeships available for young people. However, without addressing the issue of the demand for labour, any training initiative – however rigorous and effectively delivered – will never be enough.

There are various ways of increasing the demand for labour. On one level, job creation schemes such as New Labour's Future Jobs Fund can offer valuable work experience, if properly funded and effectively managed. In isolation, however, such initiatives can only have a limited impact. A far-reaching programme to create sustainable jobs is necessary in order to provide the employment opportunities needed. We agree with Allen and Ainley (2011:19) that an extensive Keynesian-style programme of public works – restoring housing, engaging in environmental initiatives, and improving local and national infrastructure –

would go some way towards bridging the opportunity gap that currently exists.

Alongside such a programme, a range of options could be used to increase the demand for skilled labour. These include statutory licences to practice across the economy; a system of levies and benefits which encourage employers to promote workforce education and training; and legislation which rewards high-quality production strategies. Such measures are not on the Government's agenda.

Deep public spending cuts can only damage the organisations most likely to deliver increased employment, and especially highly skilled employment: local authorities, universities, the health service, and other areas of the public sector. Moreover, much of the high-skill work taking place in the private sector, for example, in the pharmaceuticals and aerospace industries, is heavily subsidised by the state through the NHS and the Ministry of Defence (Atkinson and Elliott, 2007:37).

If effective measures are to be taken to improve the opportunities available to young people then a political and philosophical shift is required: free market approaches are inadequate to deal with matters of social and economic equity. The position of NEET young people is related to broader dimensions of social justice, and the need to balance the drive for profit against the needs of the workforce and well-being of local communities. The changes in taxation, labour market regulation and social policy that are necessary to achieve such ambitions would not be easy or straightforward to sustain. However, such measures are fundamental to securing socially just outcomes for young people.

Appendix 1:
Participants in the E2E project

Pseudonym	Age	Lives with	Parents' occupation as reported by participant	Completed school	GCSE A*-C	GCSE < C	Previous activities reported since leaving school
Faye	17	Mum	Working - not known	Yes	1	0	Job, college, E2E
Janice	18	Partner	Supermarket assistant	Yes	0	0	NEET, E2E, college
Kerry	18	Alone	Not stated	No	0	0	NEET, college, NEET
Amanda	17	Mum	Ironing	Yes	0	3	Apprenticeship, NEET
Jade	16	Mum	Cleaner/unemployed	Yes	0	4	Came direct to E2E
Danielle	17	Mum and Dad	British Waterways; packing factory	Yes	2	2	E2E, NEET
Ruth	17	Alone	Banking; dinner lady	Yes	2	5	NEET, private training provider, private training provider
Donna	17	Mum	Bottle packing; housewife	Yes	0	4	E2E
Yasmeena	16	Mum and Dad	Taxi driver; housewife	Yes	1	5	Missed college enrolment
Matt	17	Mum and Dad	Self-employed; administration	Yes	7	0	College

Pseudonym	Age	Lives with	Parents' occupation as reported bY participant	Completed school	GCSE A*-C	GCSE < C	Previous activities reported since leaving school
Sophie	17	Dad	Unemployed lorry driver	No	0	0	Job, college, NEET
Hannah	17	Dad	Window cleaner	Yes	8	0	School sixth form, job
Becky	17	Mum	Carer for learner so unemployed	Yes	1	2	School sixth form, NEET
Linzi	17	Mum and Dad	Unemployed	No	0	4	Private training provider
Nasreen	16	Mum and Dad	Post office; housewife	No	3	4	School sixth form
Mary	18	Mum and Dad	Both disabled – don't work	Yes	0	5	College, private training provider, job
Sean	16	Mum and Dad	Unemployed warden; working	Yes	0	3	College
Aisha	17	Mum and Dad	Data security firm	Yes	3	1	College
Jessica	17	Mum	Unemployed	No	0	0	NEET
Carl	17	Alone	Not stated	No	0	0	NEET
Charlotte	16	Mum	PT work	Yes	3	1	College, NEET

Pseudonym	Age	Lives with	Parents' occupation as reported bY participant	Completed school	GCSE A*-C	GCSE < C	Previous activities reported since leaving school
Emma	16	Mum	Restaurant owner; banking	No	0	0	NEET, college
Shannon	17	Alone	Not stated	No	0	3	College, NEET
Alan	17	Mum and Dad	Accountant; cleaner	Yes	1	4	NEET, E2E, job
Jack	17	Mum	Builder; housewife	Yes	0	5	Private training provider
Patrick	18	Mum	NHS supervisor	Yes	0	0	College
Adam	16	Mum	Not stated	Yes	0	4	Came direct to E2E
Philip	16	Mum and Dad	Not stated	Yes	0	4	Came direct to E2E
Darren	16	Mum	Not stated	Yes	5	0	Came direct to E2E
Shoaib	18	Mum and Dad	Not stated	Yes	1	2	College
Leon	16	Mum	Factory worker; hairdresser	No	0	0	NEET
Ellie	17	Mum	Unemployed – recently laid off; formerly worked in gym;	No	3	3	Came direct to E2E

Pseudonym	Age	Lives with	Parents' occupation as reported bY participant	Completed school	GCSE A*-C	GCSE < C	Previous activities reported since leaving school
Lewis	17	Relative	Sick leave; warehouse supervisor	No	0	4	NEET, Young Offenders Institution
Daniel	16	Dad	Supermarket worker	Yes	1	3	College
Joseph	17	Mum	Maternity leave	Yes	2	5	NEET
Aidan	17	Mum and Dad	Salesman; bookmakers	Yes	2	2	NEET
Rob	17	Relative	Retired	Yes	0	0	Came direct to E2E
Luke	18	Mum	Unemployed	No	0	0	College, NEET
Phil	16	Mum and Dad	Builder	Yes	1	4	NEET
Diana	18	Alone	Publican	Yes	0	4	NEET, E2E
Conal	17	Mum	Agency carer	Yes	0	1	School sixth form, NEET
Kieran	17	Mum and Dad	Engineer; hairdresser	Yes	1	3	Job, NEET
Usman	17	Mum and Dad	Textile factory; housewife	Yes	3	3	College, NEET, job

Pseudonym	Age	Lives with	Parents' occupation as reported by participant	Completed school	GCSE A*-C	GCSE < C	Previous activities reported since leaving school
Majid	17	Mum and Dad	Taxi driver; housewife	Yes	0	4	NEET
Thomas	17	Mum	Primary teacher	Yes	1	2	College, job, NEET
Mike	16	Mum	Disabled – doesn't work	No	0	0	E2E
Jason	16	Mum	Cleaner	Yes	0	0	Job
Geoffrey	17	Mum	Cleaner	No	0	2	E2E
Tom	17	Mum and Dad	Sheet metal; banking	No	0	0	Not reported
Nick	17	Alone	Unemployed fencer; supermarket assistant	No	0	3	Job
Carl	–	Mum	Carer	Yes	0	1	College, NEET

References

Ainley, P (1990) *Vocational Education and Training*. Milton Keynes: Open University Press

Ainley, P and Allen, M (2010) *Lost Generation? New strategies for youth and education*. London: Continuum

Ainley, P. and Corney, M. (1990) *Training for the Future: the rise and fall of the Manpower Services Commission*. London: Cassell

Allen, M and Ainley, P (2007) *Education make you fick, innit? What's gone wrong in England's schools, colleges and universities and how to start putting it right*. London: Tufnell

Allen, M and Ainley, P (2011) *Why Young People Can't Get the Jobs they Want: and what can be done about it*. E-booklet, http://www.radicaled.wordpress.com

Althusser, L (1971) Ideology and ideological state apparatuses, in L. Althusser, *Lenin and Philosophy and Other Essays*. London: New Left Books

Anderson, G (1990) *Fundamentals of educational research*. London: Falmer

Anderson, P (2000) Renewals. *New Left Review*, 1, p1-20

Archer, L (2008) The impossibility of minority ethnic educational 'success'? An examination of the discourses of teachers and pupils in British secondary schools. *European Educational Research Journal*, 7(1), p89-107

Archer, L, Hollingworth, S and Mendick, H (2010) *Urban Youth and Schooling*. Maidenhead: Open University Press

Armstrong, D, Istance, D, Loudon, R, McCready, S, Rees, G and Wilson, D (1997) *Status 0: A socioeconomic study of young people on the margin*. Belfast: Department of Higher and Further Education, Training and Employment

Atkinson, D and Elliott, L (2007) *Fantasy Island: waking up to the incredible economic, political and social illusions of the Blair legacy*. London: Constable

Avis, J. (2004) Work-based learning and social justice: 'learning to labour' and the new vocationalism in England. *Journal of Education and Work*, 17(2), p197-217

Avis, J (2006) Improvement through research: policy science or policy scholarship. *Research in Post-Compulsory Education*, 11(1), p107-114

Avis, J (2007) *Education, Policy and Social Justice.* London: Continuum

Baker, K (2010) http://www.personneltoday.com/articles/2010/05/27/55750/welfare-policy-to-be-overhauled-by-government.html (accessed 1st February 2011)

Ball, S (1995) Intellectuals or technicians? The urgent role of theory in educational studies. *British Journal of Educational Studies,* 43(3), p255-271

Ball, S (2003) *Class Strategies and the Educational Market: the middle class and social advantage.* London: RoutledgeFalmer

Ball, S. (2006) *Education Policy and Social Class: the selected works of Stephen J. Ball.* Abingdon: Routledge

Ball, S, Maguire, M, and Macrae, S (2000) *Choice, Pathways and Transitions Post-16: new youth, new economies in the global city.* London: Falmer.

Barham, C, Walling, A, Clancy, G, Hicks, S and Conn, S (2009) Young people and the labour market. *Economic and Labour Market Review,* 3(4), p17-29

Barysch, K (2003) *Germany – the Sick Man of Europe? Policy Brief.* London: Centre for European Reform

Bassey, M (2003) More advocacy: give autonomy back to teachers. *BERA Newsletter,* 84, p26-30

Bathmaker, A-M (2005) Hanging in or shaping a future: defining a role for vocationally related learning in a 'knowledge' society. *Journal of Education Policy* 20(1), p81-100

Baudrillard, J (1990) *Fatal Strategies.* New York: Semiotext(e)

Baudrillard (1998) *The Consumer Society: myths and structures.* London: Sage

Bauman, Z (1995) *Life in Fragments: Essays in Postmodern Morality.* Oxford: Blackwell

BBC (2011) http://www.bbc.co.uk/news/uk-12516677 (accessed 23rd February 2011)

Beck, U (1992) *The Risk Society: towards a new modernity.* London: Sage

Beck, U and Beck-Gernsheim, E (2002) *Individualization.* London: Sage

Beck, V, Fuller, A and Unwin, L (2006) Safety in stereotypes? The impact of gender and 'race' on young people's perceptions of their post-compulsory education and labour market opportunities. *British Educational Research Journal,* 32(5), p667-686

Becker, G (2006) The age of human capital. In H. Lauder, P. Brown, J. Dillabough and A. Halsey (eds) *Education, Globalization and Social Change.* Oxford: Oxford University Press

Bell, D and Blanchflower, D (2010) UK unemployment in the Great Recession. *National Institute Economic Review,* 214, p3-25

Bernstein, B (1971) On the classification and framing of educational knowledge. In M. Young (ed) *Knowledge and Control: new directions in the sociology of education.* London: Collier-Macmillan

Bernstein, B (2000) *Pedagogy, Symbolic Control and Identity: theory, research, critique. (Revised edition).* Oxford: Rowman and Littlefield

Beynon, H (1973) *Working for Ford.* London: Allen Lane.

Billett, S (2002) *Toward a workplace pedagogy: guidance, participation, and engagement*

Blunkett, D (2001) *Education into employability: the role of the DfEE in the economy*. Speech given at the Institute of Economic Affairs, London, 24 January

Bourdieu, P (1974) The school as a conservative force: scholastic and cultural inequalities, trans. by J.C. Whitehouse, in J. Eggleston (ed), *Contemporary Research in the Sociology of Education*. London: Methuen

Bourdieu, P. (1984) *Distinction*. London: Routledge

Bourdieu, P and Wacquant, L (1992) *An Invitation to Reflexive Sociology*. Cambridge: Polity Press

Brewer, J (2000) *Ethnography*. Buckingham: Open University Press

Brown, P (1987) *Schooling Ordinary Kids*. London: Tavistock

Brown, P and Hesketh, A (2004) *The Mismanagement of Talent: employability and jobs in the knowledge economy*. Oxford: Oxford University Press

Brown, P, Green, A and Lauder, H (2001) *High Skills: globalization, competitiveness and skills formation*. Oxford: Oxford University Press

Brown, P, Hesketh, A and Williams, S (2003) Employability in a knowledge-driven economy. *Journal of Education and Work* 16(2), p107-126

Brown, P, Lauder, H and Ashton, D (2008) Education, globalisation and the future of the knowledge economy. *European Journal of Educational Research*, 7(2), p131-156

Brown, P, Lauder, H and Ashton, D (2011) *The Global Auction: the broken promises of education, jobs and incomes*. Oxford: Oxford University Press

Burawoy, M (2005) American Sociological Association Presidential address: for public sociology. *British Journal of Sociology*, 56(2), p259-294

Bynner, J (2005) Rethinking the youth phase of the life-course: the case for emerging adulthood? *Journal of Youth Studies*, 8(4), p367-384

Bynner, J, Elias, P, McKnight A and Pierre G, (2002) *Young People's Changing Routes to Independence*. York: Joseph Rowntree Foundation

Bynner, J and Parsons, S (2002) Social exclusion and the transition from school to work: the case of young people not in education, employment or training (NEET). *Journal of Vocational Behavior*, 60, p289-309

Byrne, D (2005) *Social Exclusion (2nd edition)*. Maidenhead: Open University Press

Cabinet Office (2009) *Unleashing Aspiration: the panel on fair access to the professions*. London: Cabinet Office

Cameron, D. (2011) http://www.telegraph.co.uk/comment/8337239/How-we-will-release-the-grip-of-state-control.html (accessed 11 May 2011)

Cassen, R and Kingdon, G (2007) *Tackling Low Educational Achievement*. York: Joseph Rowntree Foundation

CERI (Centre for Educational Research and Innovation) (2002) *Educational Research and Development in England: background report*. London: OECD

Chatterton, P and Hollands, R (2003) *Urban Nightscapes: youth cultures, pleasure spaces and corporate power.* London: Routledge

Coffield, F, Borrill, C and Marshall, S (1986) *Growing up to the Margins: young adults in the North East.* Milton Keynes: Open University Press

Cohen, P and Ainley, P (2000) In the country of the blind? Youth studies and cultural studies in Britain. *Journal of Youth Studies,* 3(1), p79-95

Coles, B, Hutton, S, Bradshaw, J, Craig, G, Godfrey, C and Johnson, J (2002) Literature Review of the Costs of Being 'Not in Education, Employment or Training' at Age 16-18. *Research Report RR347.* London: DfES

Corney, M (2009) Unemployment more appealing than college. *Guardian Further Education,* 21st April

Coté, J and Bynner, J (2008) Changes in the transition to adulthood in the UK and Canada: the role of structure and agency in emergent adulthood. *Journal of Youth Studies,* 11(3), p251-265

DCSF (Department for Children, Schools and Families) (2009) *Investing in Potential.* Nottingham: DCSF.

DCSF (2010) *A policy update from DCSF for providers of E2E.* London: DCSF.

DCSF/ONS (DCSF/Office of National Statistics) (2009) *Youth Cohort Study and Longitudinal Study of Young People in England: The Activities and Experiences of 17-year-olds: England 2008.* London, DCSF/ONS, Statistical Bulletin B01/2009

Dennis, N, Henriques, F and Slaughter, C (1956) *Coal is Our Life: an analysis of a Yorkshire mining community.* London: Tavistock

Denzin, N and Lincoln, Y (1998) *The Landscape of Qualitative Research: theories and issues.* Thousand Oaks, CA: Sage Publications

DfE (2010a) Participation in Education, Training and Employment by 16-18 Year Olds in England, *Statistical First Release SFR18/2010.* London: DfE

DfE (Department for Education) (2010b) *The Importance of Teaching: the schools White Paper.* London: DfE

DfEE (Department for Education and Employment) (1999) *Learning to Succeed: a new framework for post-16 learning.* London: DfEE

DfES (Department for Education and Skills) (2001) *Modern Apprenticeships: the way to work. The Cassels Report.* London: DfES

DfES (2007) *Raising Expectations: staying in education and training post-16.* Norwich: HMSO

Duncan Smith, I (2010) *Universal credit: welfare that works.* Speech given at the Arlington Centre, Broadway, 11th November. Available online at http://www.dwp.gov.uk/newsroom/ministers-speeches/ (accessed 7 March 2011)

Ecclestone, K and Hayes, D (2008) *The Dangerous Rise of Therapeutic Education.* London: Routledge

Ecclestone, K (2009) Disciplining and cajoling the vulnerable self: therapeutic assessment of young people with 'complex needs'. *Lifelong Learning Revisited – What Next? Centre for Research in Lifelong Learning*, University of Stirling, 24-26 June

Elliott, A (2001) *Concepts of the Self*. Cambridge: Polity

Engels, F (1892) *The condition of the working-class in England in 1844*. Translated by Florence Kelley Wischnewetzky. London: Swan, Sonnenschein and Co.

Erlinghagen, M and Knuth, M (2010) Unemployment as an institutional construct? Structural differences in non-employment between selected European countries and the United States. *Journal of Social Policy*, 39(1), p71-94

Evans, L (2008) Professionalism, professionality and the development of education professionals. *British Journal of Educational Studies* 56(1), p20-38

Fairclough, N (2000) *New Labour, New Language*. London: Routledge

FECRDU (Further Education and Curriculum Review and Development Unit) (1978) *Experience, Reflection, Learning: suggestions for organisers of schemes of UVP*. London: FECRDU

Fergusson, R (2004) Discourses of exclusion: reconceptualising participation amongst young people. *Journal of Social Policy*, 33(2), p289-320

Finegold, D and Soskice, D (1988) The failure of training in Britain: analysis and prescription. *Oxford Review of Economic Policy* 4(1), p21-53

Finlay, I, Sheridan, M, McKay, J and Nudzor, H (2010) Young people on the margins: in need of more choices and more chances in twenty-first century Scotland. *British Educational Research Journal*, 36(5), p851-867

Finn, D (1987) *Training Without Jobs*. Basingstoke: Palgrave Macmillan

Forrest, R and Kearns, R (2001) Social cohesion, social capital and the neighbourhood. *Urban Studies*, 38(12), p2125-43

Foskett, N and Hemsley-Brown, J (2001) *Choosing Futures: young people's decision-making in education, training and career markets*. London: RoutledgeFalmer

Foucault, M (1989) *The Archaeology of Knowledge*. London: Routledge

France, A (2007) *Understanding Youth in Late Modernity*. Maidenhead: Open University Press

Francis, B and Skelton, C (2005) *Reassessing Gender and Achievement*. London: Routledge

Francis, B (2006) Heroes or zeroes? The discursive positioning of 'underachieving boys' in English neo-liberal education policy. *Journal of Education Policy*, 21(2), p187-200

Franzen, E and Kassman, A (2005) Longer-term labour market consequences of economic inactivity during young adulthood: a Swedish national cohort study. *Journal of Youth Studies*, 8(4), p403-424

Fuller, A and Unwin, L (2003) Fostering workplace learning: looking through the lens of apprenticeship. *European Educational Research Journal* 2(1), p41-55

Furlong, A and Cartmel, F (2003) Unemployment, integration and marginalisation: a comparative perspective on 18-24 year olds in Finland, Sweden, Scotland and Spain. In T. Hammer (ed) *Youth Unemployment and Social Exclusion in Europe*. Bristol: Policy Press

Furlong, A and Cartmel, F (2007) *Young People and Social Change: new perspectives*. Maidenhead: Open University Press

Furlong, A (2006) Not a very NEET solution: representing problematic labour market transitions among early school leavers. *Work, Employment and Society*, 20(3), p553-569

Furlong, A (2009) Revisiting transitional metaphors: reproducing social inequalities under the conditions of late modernity. *Journal of Education and Work* 22(5), p343-353

Geertz, C (1975) Thick description, in C. Geertz (ed) *The Interpretation of Cultures*. London: Hutchinson

Genda, Y (2007) Jobless youths and the NEET problem in Japan. *Social Science Japan Journal,* 10(1), p23-40

Giddens, A (1991) *Modernity and Self-Identity: self and society in the late modern age*. Cambridge: Polity Press

Giddens, A (1998) *The Third Way: the renewal of social democracy.* Cambridge: Polity Press

Gillborn, D (2010) The white working class, racism and respectability: victims, degenerates and interest-convergence. *British Journal of Educational Studies*, 58(1), p3-25

Gleeson, D (1983) *Youth Training and the Search for Work*. London: Routledge and Kegan Paul

Gleeson, D (1989) *The paradox of training: making progress out of crisis*. Milton Keynes: Open University Press

Gleeson, D and James, D (2007) The paradox of professionalism in English further education: a TLC project perspective. *Educational Review* 59(4), p451-467

Gleeson, D, Davies, J and Wheeler, E (2005) On the making and taking of professionalism in the further education workplace. *British Journal of Sociology of Education* 26(4), p445-460

Giddens, A (1998) *The Third Way: The Renewal of Social Democracy*. Cambridge: Polity

Godfrey, C, Hutton, S, Bradshaw, J, Coles, B, Craig, G and Johnson, J (2002) Estimating the Cost of being 'Not in Education, Employment or Training' at age 16-18. London: DfES, *Research Report RR346*

Green, A and White, R (2008) Shaped by place: young people's decisions about education, training and work. *Benefits,* 16(3), p213-24

Hall, D and Raffo, C (2004) Re-engaging 14-16 year olds with their schooling through work-related learning. *Journal of Vocational Education and Training*, 56(1), p69-79

Hammersley, M (1992) *What's Wrong with Ethnography?* Abingdon: Routledge

Hammersley, M and Atkinson, P (2007) *Ethnography: principles in practice. 3rd edition.* London: Routledge

Hansard (1994) South Glamorgan: Youth Unemployment, 1993. House of Lords Debate 20 July 1994, vol. 557, cc236-9

Harman, C (2006) http://www.socialistreview.org.uk/article.php?articlenumber=9840 (accessed February 6th 2011)

Harris, S (2007) *The Governance of Education: how neo-liberalism is transforming policy and practice.* London: Continuum

Hayes, J (2010) http://readingroom.ypla.gov.uk/ypla/ypla-john_hayes_press_release-pr-nov10-v1.pdf

Heath, A (2000) The political arithmetic tradition in the sociology of education. *Oxford Review of Education,* 26(3and4), p313-331

Heinz, W (2009) Structure and agency in transition research. *Journal of Education and Work,* 22(5), p391-404

Hillage, J and Pollard, E (1998) Employability: developing a framework for policy analysis, (*DfEE Research Briefing, no. 85*)

Hillman, K (2005) *Young People outside the Labour Force and Full-time Education: activities and profiles.* Camberwell: Australian Council for Educational Research

Hobsbawm, E. (1995) *Age of Extremes: the short twentieth century.* London: Abacus

Hodgson, A and Spours, K (2006) An analytical framework for policy engagement: the contested case of 14-19 reform in England. *Journal of Education Policy,* 21(6), p679-696

Hodkinson, P and Hodkinson, H (2004) The significance of individuals' dispositions in workplace learning: a case study of two teachers. *Journal of Education and Work* 17(2), p167-182

Hoggarth, L. and Smith. D (2004) Understanding the impact of Connexions on young people at risk. *Research Report RR 607.* Nottingham: DFES.

Hyland, T (2009) Mindfulness and the therapeutic function of education. *Journal of Philosophy of Education* 43(1), p119-131

Hyland, T and Winch, C (2007) *A Guide to Vocational education and Training.* London: Continuum

Ianelli, C and Smyth, E (2008) Mapping gender and social background differences in education and youth transitions across Europe. *Journal of Youth Studies,* 11(2), p213-232

Island Pulse (2010) http://www.islandpulse.co.uk/b2/single-work-programme-to-help-unemployed-into-work/ (accessed 1st February 2011)

Istance, D, Rees, G and Williamson, H (1994) *Young People Not in Education, Training or Employment in South Glamorgan.* Cardiff: South Glamorgan Training and Enterprise Council

195

Iverson, T (2005) *Capitalism, Democracy and Welfare.* Cambridge: Cambridge University Press

James, D and Biesta, G (2007) *Improving Learning Cultures in Further Education.* London: Routledge

James, D and Simmons, J (2007) Alternative assessment for learner engagement in a climate of performativity: lessons from an English case study. *Assessment in Education* 14(3), p353-371

Jeffs, T and Smith, M (1998) The problem of 'youth' for youth work. *Youth and Policy,* 62, p45-66

Jephcote, M and Salisbury, J (2009) Further education teachers' accounts of their professional identities. *Teaching and Teacher Education* 25, p966-972

Jephcote, M, Salisbury, J and Rees, G (2008) Being a teacher in further education in changing times. *Research in Post-Compulsory Education* 13(2), p163-172

Jones, G (1995) *Leaving Home.* Milton Keynes: Open University Press

Jones, G (2009) *Youth.* Cambridge: Polity Press

Keeley, G, Burke, J and Kington, T (2008) After the baby boomers, meet the children dubbed 'baby losers'. *Observer,* May 11

Keep, E (2006) State control of the English education and training system – playing with the biggest train set in the world. *Journal of Vocational Education and Training,* 58(1), p47-64

Keep, E (2009) *Employers and the Labour market: key to future progress 14-19.* Nuffield Review of 14-19 Education and Training in England and Wales Conference, 2009. University of London, Institute of Education, 22 September

Kelly, S and Price, H (2009) Vocational education: a clean slate for disengaged students? *Social Science Research*, 38, p810-825

Lansley, S (2009) *Life in the Middle: the untold story of Britain's average earners.* London: TUC

Lash, S (1992) *Modernity and Identity.* Oxford: Blackwell

Lauder, H, Brown, P, Dillabough, J, and Halsey, A (2006) The prospects for education: individualization, globalization and social change, in H. Lauder, P. Brown, J. Dillabough and A. Halsey (eds) *Education, globalization and social change.* Oxford: Oxford University Press

Lave, J and Wenger, E (1991) *Situated Learning: legitimate peripheral participation.* New York: Cambridge University Press

Leadbeater, C (2004) *Learning about Personalisation: how can we put the learner at the heart of the education system.* London: DfES

Leitch, A (2006) *Prosperity for All in the Global Economy – world class skills.* Norwich: HMSO

Levitas, R (2005) *The Inclusive Society? Social exclusion and New Labour. 2nd Edition.* Basingstoke: Palgrave Macmillan

196

Lindsay, C (2002) Long-term unemployment and the 'employability gap': priorities for renewing Britain's New Deal. *Journal of European Industrial Training,* 26(9), p411-419

Lucas, N and Unwin, L (2009) Developing teacher expertise at work: in-service trainee teachers in colleges of further education in England. *Journal of Further and Higher Education,* 33(4), 423-33

LLUK (Lifelong Learning UK) (2010) *Work Based Learning Workforce in England: factsheet for 2008-2009.* London: LLUK

LSC (Learning and Skills Council) (2006) *The Framework for Entry to Employment Programmes (Issue 2).* Coventry: LSC

LSDA (Learning and Skills Development Agency) (2003) *A summary of the E2E learning framework.* London: LSDA

MacDonald, R and Marsh, J (2001) Disconnected Youth? *Journal of Youth Studies,* 4(4), p373-391

MacDonald, R and Marsh, J (2005) *Disconnected youth? Growing up in Britain's poor neighbourhoods.* Basingstoke: Palgrave Macmillan

MacDonald, R, Shildrick, T, Webster, C and Simpson, D (2005) Growing up in poor neighbourhoods: the significance of class and place in the extended transitions of 'socially excluded' young adults. *Sociology,* 39(5), p873-891

Maffesoli, M (1996) *The Time of Tribes: The decline of individualism in mass society.* London: Sage

Maguire, S (2008) Paying young people to learn – does it work? *Research in Post-Compulsory Education,* 13(2), p205-215

Maguire, S and Thompson, J (2007) Young people not in education, employment or training (NEET) – Where is government policy taking us now? *Youth and Policy,* 8(3), p5-18

Maguire, S *et al* (2009) Activity Agreement Pilots: process evaluation. *Research Report DCSF-RR095.* London: DCSF

Mather, K, Worrall, L and Seifert, R (2007) Reforming further education: the changing labour process for college lecturers. *Personnel Review,* 36(1), p109-127

McKendrick, J, Scott, G and Sinclair, S (2007) Dismissing disaffection: young people's attitudes towards education, employment and participation in a deprived community. *Journal of Youth Studies,* 10(2), p139-160

McRae, H (1994) Too young and too precious to waste. *The Independent,* 12 May 1994

Miles, S (2000) *Youth Lifestyles in a Changing World.* Buckingham: Open University Press

Mizen, P (2004) *The Changing State of Youth.* Basingstoke: Palgrave Macmillan

Moore, R (2004) *Education and Society: issues and explanations in the sociology of education.* Cambridge: Polity Press

Munn, P and Lloyd, G (2005) Exclusion and excluded pupils. *British Educational Research Journal,* 31(2), p205-221

Murad, N (2002) The shortest way out of work. In P. Chamberlayne, M. Rustin and T. Wengraf (eds), *Biography and Social Exclusion in Europe*. Bristol: Policy Press

Mann, C (1998) The impact of working-class mothers on their adolescent daughters at a time of social change. *British Journal of Sociology of Education*, 19(2), p211-226

Murray, C (1990) *The Emerging British Underclass*. London: IEA

Murray, C (1994) *The Underclass: the crisis deepens*. London: IEA

Nayak, A (2003) 'Boyz to men', masculinities, schooling and labour transitions in de-industrial times. *Education Review*, 55(2), p147-59

Nayak, A (2006) Displaced masculinities: chavs, youth and class in the post-industrial city. *Sociology*, 40(5), p813-831

NFER (National Foundation for Educational Research) (2009) Increasing Participation: understanding young people who do not participate in education or training at 16 and 17. *Research Report DCSF-RR072*. Nottingham: DCSF

NFER (2010) Barriers to Participation in Education and Training. *Research Report DFE-RR009*. London: DCSF

OECD (2010) Off to a Good Start? Jobs for Youth. OECD position paper, available online at http://www.oecd.org/dataoecd/0/34/46717876.pdf (accessed 15 July 2011)

Orr, K and Simmons, R (2010) Dual identities: the in-service teacher trainee experience in the English further education sector. *Journal of Vocational Education and Training*, 62(1), p75-88

Parekh, A, MacInnes, T and Kenway, P (2010) *Monitoring poverty and social exclusion 2010*. York: Joseph Rowntree Foundation

Payne, J (1999) *Young People Not in Education, Employment and Training: data from the England and Wales Youth Cohort Study*. London: PSI

Payne, J (2003) *Choice at the end of compulsory schooling: a research review*. Nottingham: DfES

Peck, J. (2001) *Workfare States*. New York: Guildford

Perry, E and Francis, B (2010) T*he Social Class Gap for Educational Achievement: A review of the literature*. London: Royal Society for the Arts

Pearce, N and Hillman, J (1998) *Wasted Youth: Raising achievement and tackling social exclusion*. London: Institute for Public Policy Research

Reay, D and Lucey, H (2004) Stigmatised choices: social class, social exclusion and secondary school markets in the inner city. *Pedagogy, Culture and Society*, 12(1), p35-51

Reay, D (2002) Shaun's story: troubling discourses of white working class masculinities. *Gender and Education*, 14(3), p221-234

Reay, D (2007) 'Unruly places': inner-city comprehensives, middle-class imaginaries and working-class children. *Urban Studies*, 44(7), p1191-1201

Rees, G, Williamson, H and Istance, D (1996) 'Status Zero': a study of jobless school-leavers in South Wales. *Research Papers in Education,* 11(2), p219-235

Roberts, K (2009a) Opportunity structures then and now. *Journal of Education and Work* 22(5), p355-368

Roberts, K (2009b) *Youth in Transition: Eastern Europe and the West.* Basingstoke: Palgrave Macmillan

Robson, J (2006) *Teacher Professionalism in Further and Higher Education.* London: Routledge

Rudd, P and Evans, K (1998) Structure and agency in youth transitions: student experiences of vocational further education. *Journal of Youth Studies*, 1(1), 39-62

Russell, L, Simmons, R and Thompson, R (2010) Playing the numbers game: Connexions personal advisers working with learners on Entry to Employment programmes. *Journal of Vocational Education and Training*, 62(1), p1-12

Russell, L, Simmons, R and Thompson, R (2011) Ordinary lives: an ethnographic study of young people attending Entry to Employment programmes. *Journal of Education and Work*, forthcoming

Savelsberg, H and Martin-Giles, B (2008) Young people on the margins: Australian studies of social exclusion. *Journal of Youth Studies*, 11(1), p17-31

Scarpetta, S, Sonnet, A and Manfredi, T (2010) Rising Youth Unemployment during the Crisis: how to prevent negative long-term consequences on a generation. *OECD Social, Employment and Migration Papers*, No. 106. Paris: OECD.

Scottish Executive (2006) *More choices, more chances: a strategy to reduce the proportion of young people not in education, employment or training in Scotland.* Edinburgh: Scottish Executive

SEU (Social Exclusion Unit) (1999) *Bridging the Gap: New opportunities for 16-18 year olds not in Education, Employment or Training.* London: The Stationery Office, Cm4405

Shain, F (2003) *The Schooling and Identity of Asian Girls.* Stoke-on-Trent: Trentham Books

Shain, F and Gleeson, D (1999) Under new management: changing conceptions of teacher professionalism and policy in the further education sector. *Journal of Education Policy* 14(4), p445-462

Shildrick, T and MacDonald, R (2007) Biographies of exclusion: poor work and poor transitions *International Journal of Lifelong Education* 26(5), p589-604

Shildrick, T, MacDonald, R, Webster, C and Garthwaite, K (2010) *The low-pay, no-pay cycle: understanding recurrent poverty.* York: Joseph Rowntree Foundation

Simmons, R (2008) Raising the age of compulsory education in England: A NEET solution? *British Journal of Educational Studies*, 56(4), p420-439

Simmons, R (2009) Entry to employment: discourses of inclusion and employability in work-based learning for young people. *Journal of Education and Work*, 22(2), p137-151

Smith, A. (1785) *An Enquiry into the Nature and Causes of the Wealth of Nations* London: Strahan, Cadell and Davies

Social Exclusion Task Force (2009) *Understanding the Risks of Social Exclusion across the Life Course: youth and young adulthood.* London: Cabinet Office

Spielhofer, T *et al* (2009) *Increasing participation: understanding young people who do not participate in education and training at 16 and 17.* Nottingham: DCSF Publications

Spielhofer, T, Mann, P and Sims, D (2003) *Entry to Employment (E2E) participant study.* London: LSDA

Steinert, H (2003) Participation and social exclusion: a conceptual framework, in H. Steinert and A. Pilgram (eds) *Welfare Policy from Below: struggles against social exclusion in Europe.* Aldershot: Ashgate

Thompson, R (2010) Teaching on the margins: tutors, discourse and pedagogy in work-based learning for young people. *Journal of Vocational Education and Training* 62(2), p123-137

Thompson, R (2011a) Reclaiming the disengaged? A Bourdieuian analysis of work-based learning for young people in England. *Critical Studies in Education*, 52(1), p15-28

Thompson, R (2011b) Individualisation and social exclusion: the case of young people not in education, employment or training. *Oxford Review of Education*, 62(6), forthcoming

Thompson, R and Robinson, D (2008) Changing step or marking time? Teacher education reforms for the learning and skills sector in England. *Journal of Further and Higher Education* 32(2), p161-173

Thomson, P and Russell, L (2009) Data, data everywhere – but not all the numbers that count? Mapping alternative provisions for students excluded from school. *International Journal of Inclusive Education* 13(4), p423-438

Tomlinson, M (2007) Graduate employability and student attitudes and orientations to the labour market. *Journal of Education and Work*, 20(4), p285-304

Tooley, J and Darby, D (1998) *Educational research: a critique.* London: Ofsted

Tusting, K and Barton, P (2007) *Programmes for unemployed people since the 1970s: the changing place of language, literacy and numeracy.* London: National Research and Development Centre for Adult Literacy and Numeracy

Turner, R (2000) *Coal Was Our Life.* Sheffield: Sheffield Hallam University Press

UCU (2011) http://www.ucu.org.uk/index.cfm?articleid=5236 (accessed January 27th 2011)

Veit-Wilson, J (1998) *Setting Adequacy Standards.* Bristol: Policy Press

Wacquant, L (1999) Urban marginality in the coming millennium. *Urban Studies*, 36(10), p1639-1647

Walford, G (2009) For ethnography. *Ethnography and Education*, 4(3), p271-282

Wheelahan, L (2009) The problem with CBT (and why constructivism makes things worse). *Journal of Education and Work* 22(3), p227-242

Whitty, G. (2001) Education, social class and social exclusion. *Journal of Education Policy*, 16, p287-95

Wilkinson, C (1995) *The Drop Out Society: young people on the margin.* Leicester: Youth Work Press

Williamson, H (2010) Neet acronym is far from a neat description. *TES Cymru*, 5 March 2010. Available online at http://www.tes.co.uk/article.aspx?storycode=6038266

Willis, P (1977) *Learning to Labour: How working-class kids get working-class jobs.* London: Ashgate

Willis, P (1983) Cultural production and theories of reproduction, in: Barton, L. and Walker, S. (eds) *Race, Class and Education.* London: Croom-Helm

Wilson, W and Wacquant, L (1989) The cost of racial and class exclusion in the inner city. *Annals of the American Academy of Social and Political Science*, 501, p5-25

Wilson, W (1992) Another look at 'the truly disadvantaged'. *Political Science Quarterly*, 106, p.639-656

Wolf, A (2002) *Does Education Matter? Myths about education and economic growth.* London: Penguin

Wolf, A (2011) *Review of Vocational Education – The Wolf Report.* London: Department for Education

Wright-Mills, C (1959) *The Sociological Imagination.* Oxford: Oxford University Press

Yates, S and Payne, M (2006) Not so NEET? A critique of the use of 'NEET' in setting targets for interventions with young people. *Journal of Youth Studies*, 9(3), p329-344

Yates, S, Harris, A, Sabates, R and Staff, J (2010) Early occupational aspirations and fractured transitions: a study of entry into NEET status in the UK. *Journal of Social Policy*, 40(3), p1-22

Young, M and Willmott, P (1962) *Family and Kinship in East London.* Penguin: Harmondsworth

Index